Understanding the Corporate Annual Report: Nuts, Bolts, and a Few Loose Screws is a must for anybody concerned with safeguarding financial resources. There is simply no other book on the market that helps you to fully understand and comprehend the corporate annual report in such a readable, easy to understand, step-by-step manner. This is what people are saying:

"This book clarifies the complexity of annual reports. Now I understand how to evaluate what they say and can decide more confidently where to invest for my retirement"

—Stephen Biles, Program Manager, Dell Computer

"In view of the Enron disaster, more responsibility for making investment decisions will be placed in the hands of the individual investor. . . . In just a few hours, the Fraser/Ormiston book can quickly educate investors how to evaluate the performance of companies in order to make more financially astute decisions. It's a 'must read' for anyone either starting to invest or for anyone who has used the 'dart-board' approach to investing."

—Dianne R. Morrison, Finance Professor, University of Wisconsin–La Crosse

Visit the Web site at www.prenhall.com/fraser

Understanding the Corporate Annual Report

Understanding the Corporate Annual Report

Nuts, Bolts, and a Few Loose Screws

Lyn M. Fraser

Aileen Ormiston

Prentice Hall

Upper Saddle River, New Jersey 07458

Library of Congress Cataloging-in-Publication

Fraser, Lyn M.
    Understanding the corporate annual report : nuts, bolts, and a few loose screws / Lyn M.
    Fraser, Aileen Ormiston
        p.cm.
    Includes bibliographical references and index.
    ISBN 0-13-100431-X
      1. Corporation reports. 2. Financial statements. 3. Corporation reports—United States.
    4. Financial statements—United States. I. Title: Corporate annual report. II. Ormiston,
    Aileen. III. Title.

HG4028.B2 F73 2003
332.63'2042—dc21   2002073952

Acquisitions Editor: Thomas Sigel
Editor-in-Chief: P. J. Boardman
Assistant Editor: Jessica Romeo
Editorial Assistant: Linda Albelli
Marketing Manager: Beth Toland
Marketing Assistant: Christine Genneken
Managing Editor (Production): John Roberts
Production Editor: Renata Butera
Permissions Coordinator: Suzanne Grappi
Associate Director, Manufacturing: Vincent Scelta
Production Manager: Arnold Vila
Manufacturing Buyer: Michelle Klein
Cover Design and Illustration: Jerry McDaniel
Composition: Carlisle Communications, Ltd.
Full-Service Project Management: Carlisle Communications, Ltd.
Printer/Binder: Courier Kendallville

Credits and acknowledgments borrowed from other sources and reproduced, with permission, in this
textbook appear on the appropriate page within text.

Pearson Education LTD.
Pearson Education Australia PTY, Limited
Pearson Education Singapore, Pte. Ltd.
Pearson Education North Asia Ltd.
Pearson Education, Canada, Ltd.
Pearson Educación de Mexico, S.A. de C.V.
Pearson Education–Japan
Pearson Education Malaysia, Pte. Ltd

10 9 8 7 6 5 4 3 2
ISBN 0-13-100431-X

For Eleanor.
The book quite literally would not
have happened without her.
—Lyn M. Fraser

This book is dedicated to all
users of annual reports.
—Aileen Ormiston

BRIEF CONTENTS

CONTENTS

PREFACE

It is increasingly evident that those who rely on reported financial information—such as investors, creditors, employees, suppliers, customers, and competitors—cannot depend exclusively on the reports of so-called "independent" auditors or on the recommendations of market analysts in evaluating a company's financial health and prospects. To make informed choices, those involved in financial decision-making need a basic understanding of a company's financial reports and the ability to evaluate the information they contain.

The primary resource for assessing a company's financial condition and performance is the set of financial statements, notes, management discussion, auditors' report, and other information presented in its annual report to shareholders. (The companion documents to the corporate annual report are the 10-K report filed annually and the 10-Q reports filed quarterly with the Securities and Exchange Commission.) The purpose of this book is to help readers understand and evaluate the information presented in a corporate annual report for purposes of making financial decisions relating to that company.

HOW THIS BOOK CAN HELP

This book provides a clearly written, step-by-step guide through the corporate annual report. The authors show readers how to cut through the window dressing and attempts by management to manipulate earnings and other performance measures. They explain what the numbers and other information mean for purposes of making practical business decisions. Examples based on actual company reports are used throughout the book. The material is presented on a level that can be read and understood by any reader—regardless of background—who is interested in making sense of the information contained in a corporate annual report.

Chapter 1 lays out the basic content of an **annual report,** discusses what to use and what to ignore, and provides a personal example of how the approach taken in the book can help readers. The personal example is based on the experience of one of the book's authors and her daughter, who worked at Enron Corporation (and did not lose her 401(k) investment).

Chapter 2 provides a brief introduction to accounting methods, takes readers step-by-step through the **statement of earnings (income statement),** discusses various measures of "earnings," and shows readers how to assess the quality of reported earnings by illustrating techniques for earnings management and abuses in the recognition of revenue, expenses, and profits.

Chapter 3 covers the **statement of financial condition (balance sheet)** and the **statement of shareholders' equity,** including the accounting principles and management choices that affect their presentation.

Chapter 4 discusses the **statement of cash flows** with a focus on **cash flow from operations** (and related analytical concepts) to measure performance.

Chapter 5 shows readers how to utilize the material in a corporate annual report for practical decision-making by presenting a comprehensive analysis using financial ratios and other analytical tools; the chapter also discusses additional resources for evaluating company reports.

Throughout the book, examples are based on actual company reports. The 2000 Annual Report for Eastman Kodak Company provides the basic background, and other companies' reports are used to illustrate specific additional issues.

Each chapter includes a list of caution flags relating to the material presented in the chapter. The caution flags are useful in highlighting areas that require additional analysis and in helping readers spot potential problems. A supplement to Chapter 5 illustrates how the caution flags could have been used to identify problems in the WorldCom Inc. 2001 annual report.

A Test Yourself section is available at the conclusion of each chapter (with Solutions at the end of the book), offering an opportunity for readers to assess comprehension of the material presented.

A Glossary of key terms used throughout the book is also provided. To assist readers in selecting material that is relevant to particular areas of interest, the topics covered in each chapter are listed immediately following the chapter title. Some of the more complicated accounting explanations (relating to issues such as accounting for investments, accounting for deferred taxes, keeping debt off the books, accounting for leases, stock dividends and stock splits, and financial leverage) are presented separately in a box within the appropriate chapter.

A Note About Errors

The authors and publishers have made every effort to provide an error-free publication. In the event readers do find mistakes, however, one of the book's authors, Lyn Fraser, would like to offer a brief word of explanation and apology. First, if there are errors, they are in all probability *not* the fault of Aileen Ormiston. Lyn Fraser had the ultimate responsibility for correcting mistakes. Unfortunately, whenever Lyn sat down at her computer to correct the errors that had been found by Aileen and others in the review process, Lyn's cat R. T. took it upon himself to participate fully in the tedious error-correcting sessions. He paced back and forth between the computer and printer, yelping "Ack, Ack." He would sit briefly on the printer cable, then march triumphantly across the computer keyboard. If readers find something in the book that looks like this: dezsssmmmmmmmm9iiiiiddddddddddddddddddddddddddddddddddddddrt, it is the work of R. T.'s creative paws.

ACKNOWLEDGMENTS

The authors would like to acknowledge the help of those who made the writing and publication of this book possible. Specifically, Lyn would like to thank Eleanor Fraser, Reenie Neal, Muffie Moroney, T. L. Waters, Derby Hirst, Ruthie, and the aforementioned R. T. for a variety of enormously helpful contributions to the planning and writing process.

Aileen would like to thank Michael and Joshua Ormiston for their helpful comments. She also thanks her sister, Kathy Kuebbing, for the inspiring question sent to her in a letter—"Can you revise your financial statements book to include a chapter on Enron-like behavior?" And finally, she thanks all her family members for not feeling too neglected as she spent time with "nuts, bolts, and a few loose screws."

Both authors express grateful appreciation to their editor, Thomas Sigel, for his vision, support, and sense of humor; and to Annie Todd, Beth Toland, and the many others in the editorial, production, and marketing departments of Prentice Hall for their assistance at each stage of the writing and production process. Renata Butera of Prentice Hall and Ann Imhof of Carlisle Communications have handled the book's production with great patience and consideration.

We especially thank the following people who reviewed and commented on the manuscript prior to publication: Stephen Biles, Dell Computer; Frederick Deal, General Dynamics; Dianne Morrison, University of Wisconsin–La Crosse; and Nancy B. Rapoport, University of Houston Law Center.

This book reflects a collaboration between the two authors that began in the early 1980s at Texas A&M University. It has spanned two decades and six editions of the authors' other Prentice Hall book, *Understanding Financial Statements*. The authors share a commitment to quality that we hope is reflected in this new book, *Understanding the Corporate Annual Report: Nuts, Bolts, and a Few Loose Screws.* We also hope readers find this book accessible, helpful, and perhaps even enjoyable.

Lyn M. Fraser
Aileen Ormiston

About the Authors

Lyn M. Fraser has taught undergraduate and graduate classes in financial statement analysis at Texas A&M University and has conducted numerous seminars on the subject for executive development and continuing education courses. A Certified Public Accountant, she is the co-author with Aileen Ormiston of *Understanding Financial Statements* (Prentice Hall, 6th edition, 2001) and has published articles in the *Journal of Accountancy,* the *Journal of Commercial Bank Lending,* the *Magazine of Bank Administration,* and the *Journal of Business Strategies.* She has been recognized for Distinguished Achievement in Teaching by the Former Students Association at Texas A&M University and is a member of Phi Beta Kappa.

Aileen Ormiston teaches accounting in the Business Department of Mesa Community College in Mesa, Arizona. She received her bachelor's degree in accounting from Michigan State University and a master's degree in finance from Texas A&M University. She is a member of the American Institute of Certified Public Accountants, the Accounting Association, and the Institute of Management Accountants. Mesa Community College was one of 13 universities and colleges that received a grant from the Accounting Education Change Commission, and Aileen was actively involved in developing the new accounting curriculum.

The authors' book, *Understanding Financial Statements,* has sold more than 140,000 copies.

Chapter 1

I Told My Daughter Not to Invest in Enron

➤ *The financial reporting environment*

➤ *Corporate annual reports—regulation*

➤ *Contents of a corporate annual report—what's important, what's not*

➤ *A personal story from one of the book's co-authors*

➤ *Caution flags for users of annual reports*

➤ *Test yourself*

In the collapse of Enron Corporation, which filed in December 2001 for the largest bankruptcy in U.S. history, investors, creditors, and employees experienced a financial free-fall that had been essentially missed (or misrepresented) not only by its auditors, but by security analysts as well. Although not as dramatic and devastating, there have been numerous predecessors and successors to Enron's demise—a long list of company failings and failures that have had disastrous effects on shareholders, employees, and creditors.

These developments have occurred over a period of dramatic increase in the percentage of individuals who now invest in corporate stocks and bonds, many through 401(k) plans and Individual Retirement Accounts (IRAs). For example, it is estimated that by year-end 2000, 42 million Americans held 401(k) plan accounts with $1.8 trillion in assets.[1] Obviously, these accounts are intended to be a major source of retirement income for U.S. households, now and in the future.

---

[1] Sarah Holden and Jack VanDerhei, "401(k) Plan Asset Allocation, Account Balances, and Loan Activity in 2000," *EBRI Issue Brief* (Washington, D.C.: Employee Benefit Research Institute, November 2001), p. 3.

1

THE FINANCIAL REPORTING ENVIRONMENT

The current environment for financial reporting is one in which companies are under extreme pressure to produce rising sales and earnings in order to meet projected earnings targets, corporate executive compensation packages are frequently tied to company performance, and employees have increasingly large stakes in the firm's common stock. Companies have found endlessly creative ways to

- overstate earnings with aggressive revenue measurement techniques,
- confuse readers about what "profit" measures to use,
- report steadily rising profits while failing to generate any cash from operations,
- make future performance look better by taking huge lump-sum write-offs currently,
- smooth reported earnings by boosting or delaying revenue and expenses, and
- keep debt off the balance sheet and hidden in footnotes.

Even practices that are legal and acceptable on an item-by-item basis according to the guidelines established by accounting rule-makers often produce a distorted overall picture of the firm's financial condition and performance.

Auditors

Auditors' reports are intended to provide an objective statement about the fairness of corporate financial statements, but the numerous cases and judgments against auditing firms in recent years have resulted in skepticism about reliance on the so-called "independence" of auditors. Questions relate to such issues as auditors being aware of problems but giving clean auditing reports anyway, accounting firms providing lucrative consulting as well as auditing functions for a company, and situations in which the financial officers responsible for preparing a company's financial statements previously worked for the accounting firm providing the audit. At midyear 2001, the Securities and Exchange Commission had more than 250 accounting investigations in process, including 40 of the 500 largest firms in the country.[2] The problems with auditors are discussed in more detail later in this chapter.

Analysts

The analysts who study publicly traded companies and make recommendations to investors have also been brought into question.[3] Public confidence has been shaken by the hyping of marginal companies during the boom in dot-com company stocks and by overly optimistic recommendations by analysts in the midst of severe market downturns. For example, at one point during a 2000 market slide when one of the major market indexes, the NASDAQ, was down 60 percent, fewer than 1 percent of

---

[2] Michael Shroeder, "SEC List of Accounting-Fraud Probe Grows," *The Wall Street Journal* (July 6, 2001), p. C4.

[3] Scott Thurm and Charles Gasparino, "When Do Analysts Cover Their Own Interests?" *The Wall Street Journal* (December 10, 2001), p. C1.

analysts' recommendations were to sell.[4] Amidst growing criticism that some analysts are not independent of the companies they tout, the Securities and Exchange Commission issued an Investor Alert, "Analyzing Analyst Recommendations," to warn investors to treat analysts' advice with caution.

The alert points out that the analysts who advise investors may themselves have conflicts of interest such as holding shares in the companies they recommend and working for firms that underwrite securities. Although analysts are an important source of information in today's complex markets, the Securities and Exchange Commission's alert encourages investors considering whether to buy, hold, or sell a security not to rely solely on an analyst's advice but rather to research the company by studying its financial reports.[5] The authors of this book certainly agree with that suggestion.

To make informed choices, it is increasingly evident that those who rely on reported financial information need a basic understanding of company financial reports and the ability to evaluate the material they contain. The objective of this book is to help readers do exactly that—to decipher what's in a corporate annual report and use the information to make practical financial decisions.

ANNUAL REPORTS: REGULATION

Any discussion of financial reports must begin with an introduction to the principles that underlie their preparation and the institutions responsible for specifying and regulating their content. The preparation of financial statements and their accompanying information are based on **generally accepted accounting principles (GAAP)**, which have evolved through a combination of stated rules or pronouncements issued by regulatory authorities and sometimes by the actual accounting practices used by companies. These principles are intended to achieve a presentation of financial information that is understandable for users and relevant to decision-making. The objective of GAAP is to ensure that a company's reports of its financial condition and performance reflect economic reality.

The two authorities primarily responsible for establishing GAAP in the United States are the **Securities and Exchange Commission (SEC)** in the public sector and the **Financial Accounting Standards Board (FASB)** in the private sector. In recent years, the U.S. Congress has also played a role in exerting political influence on accounting policies relating to such issues as accounting for stock options, goodwill, and the debate over potential accounting fraud stimulated by the collapse of Enron.

Securities and Exchange Commission

The SEC regulates companies that issue securities to the public and requires the issuance of a prospectus for any new security offerings as well as regular filings of

---

4   Associated Press, "Public warned about analysts," *Arizona Republic* (June 29, 2001), p. D3.
5   Securities and Exchange Commission, "Analyzing Analyst Recommendations," *Investor Alert, 2001.* Available at www.sec.gov/investor/pubs/analysts.htm.

annual reports **(10-K),** quarterly reports **(10-Q)**, and other reports (filed as **8-K)** dependent upon particular circumstances such as a change in auditor, bankruptcy, or other important events. The SEC also requires public companies to solicit shareholder votes in a document called the **proxy statement,** because many stockholders do not attend shareholder meetings. The proxy statement contains information about the company's nominated directors and recommended auditor as well as figures on the compensation for a company's highest five paid executives and any proposed changes in compensation plans. This information can be extremely useful in assessing the quality of a company's management. These reports required by the SEC are available to the public and can be accessed for most companies on the Web at www.edgar-online.com.

Through the Securities Exchange Act of 1934, the SEC was granted statutory authority to set accounting and reporting standards, and the SEC has issued rulings called "Accounting Series Releases" and "Financial Report Rulings." The SEC also plays an oversight role in attempting to assure that companies' actual accounting practices follow stated principles. The degree of aggressiveness with which the SEC pursues offenders has ebbed and flowed over the years. Under the leadership of Arthur Levitt (SEC chair 1993–2001), who declared war on "earnings management," the SEC was intensely aggressive in bringing action against companies suspected of accounting irregularities.[6] Harvey Pitt was appointed to the chairmanship in 2001, perhaps signaling a shift in tone, as indicated by such policies as allowing companies to avoid penalties by reporting their own misdeeds.[7] In response to the Enron crisis and failed audits at other major companies, Pitt has proposed forming an independent group to oversee audits of public companies.

Financial Accounting Standards Board

For the most part, the SEC's policy has been to rely on the private sector for the setting of financial accounting and reporting standards. Since its creation in 1973, this function has been provided by the Financial Accounting Standards Board. The FASB is comprised of seven full-time, paid members. The board issues "Statements of Financial Accounting Standards and Interpretations," usually after a lengthy process of deliberation with input from accounting firms, the companies and industries affected by prospective rulings, representatives from government, and the general public. The FASB has issued more than 140 Statements of Financial Accounting Standards; information about the FASB, a summary of issued statements, and a list of exposure drafts outstanding can be accessed on the Web at www.fasb.org.

The process of establishing accounting policy is adversarial in the sense that those preparing the financial statements—the companies—often have entirely different objectives from those using the information—such as shareholders and lenders. Some accounting pronouncements have been significantly altered in the review and revision period as a result of intense lobbying by corporations.

---

[6] Carol J. Loomis, "Lies, Damned Lies, and Managed Earnings," *Fortune* (August 2, 1999), pp. 74–90.
[7] Michael Schroeder and Jonathan Weil, "SEC Chooses a More Lenient Tack," *The Wall Street Journal* (October 24, 2001), p. C1.

Other Agencies

Prior to the creation of the FASB, accounting policy was set primarily by the American Institute of Certified Public Accountants (AICPA), which still plays a major role through participation in the FASB policy-making process and by the setting of standards used for auditing, called "Statements of Auditing Standards (SAS)." To address the globalization of business activity, the International Accounting Standards Committee (IASC) was established in 1973; the IASC formulates international accounting policies and works closely with the SEC and FASB.

ANNUAL REPORT CONTENT: NUTS, BOLTS, AND A FEW LOOSE SCREWS

Annual reports in this book refer to the information published primarily for shareholders and the general public by more than 12,000 companies. These documents are mailed each year to shareholders and are available by request from the company's investor relations department; for most companies, they can also be accessed on the Web and either read or downloaded from the company's Web site. The 10-K report required by the SEC for large publicly held companies is also an annual report, somewhat more detailed and widely used by regulators, analysts, and researchers. The basic set of financial statements and supplementary information is the same for both documents.[8] The 10-Q, or quarterly report, filed with the SEC provides information about a firm's financial condition and performance between annual report filings; the quarterly reports are unaudited.

The annual reports discussed in the book apply to most industries except those that have specialized accounting rules (e.g., banks and utilities); even for those industries, however, many of the issues covered in the book apply. The book is also helpful in evaluating the financial reports of small companies—those that are not publicly traded—provided that they follow generally accepted accounting principles.

The material contained in an annual report typically includes the following items:

- Impressive front cover
- Colored photographs on shiny paper with images of the company's business operations, its satisfied employees and customers, the smiling chief executive officer (CEO), chief financial officer (CFO), and possibly the entire board of directors
- Dazzling graphics demonstrating the company's successes
- Letter to shareholders with positive spin

---

[8] The 10-K report includes sections on Business; Properties; Legal Proceedings; Submission of Matters to a Vote of Security Holders; Market for Registrant's Common Equity and Related Stockholder Matters; Selected Financial Data; Management's Discussion and Analysis of Financial Condition and Results of Operations; Financial Statements and Supplementary Data; Changes in and Disagreements with Accountants on Accounting and Financial Disclosure; Directors and Executive Officers of the Registrant; Executive Compensation; Security Ownership of Certain Beneficial Owners and Management; Certain Relationships and Related Transactions; Exhibits, Financial Statement Schedules, and Reports on Form 8-K.

- Four financial statements—the statement of earnings (income statement); statement of financial condition (balance sheet); statement of shareholders' equity; and the statement of cash flows
- Notes to the financial statements
- Report of independent auditors
- Management's discussion and analysis
- Five-year summary of selected financial data—net sales or operating revenue; income or loss from continuing operations; income or loss from continuing operations per common share; total assets; long-term obligations and redeemable preferred stock; and cash dividends per common share
- Market data—high and low sales prices on common stock each quarter for the past 2 years

Readers can probably come up with their own ranking of usefulness for the above items that comprise annual reports. The content that is *required* by regulators for inclusion consists of the last six items—the financial statements, notes, auditor's report, management's discussion, the 5-year summary of key figures, and the market data—and they will be the focus of this book. The other material is presented at the discretion of management and packaged to make the company appealing to current and prospective investors, employees, and customers. Some of these same creations also show up on corporate Web sites.

Slick Stuff

The public relations additions (first four items) to the financial presentations, while appealing, sometimes make the needed information difficult to find. This material may even backfire, leading to skepticism on the part of astute readers. For example, Time Warner reported net losses for all 3 years on the earnings statement of its 1998 annual report. Finding the financial statement required leafing through 32 pages of glossy pictures and other information about the entertainment industry. In a year in which Bristol Myers-Squibb reported a 17 percent *increase* in profits, the annual report had 63 pages—40 pages of fluff and 23 of financial reports. The following year, 1989, the company's earnings *decreased* by 40 percent; the annual report had 78 slick-paper pages with 32 full-page color photos, and the same 23 pages of financial information. The ratio of fluff to financial data was more than 3:1 in the bad year compared with less than 2:1 in the good year. Enron's 1999 annual report shows single photos of its entire board of directors in relaxed, almost dancing postures. Not surprisingly, many 2001 annual reports have been toned down to reflect not only the year's economy but also the events of September 11 and its aftermath.

Letter to Shareholders

The attempts by a company's chair/CEO to "spin" in shareholder letters sometimes border on dark comedy:

1. The Chairman and CEO of Lucent Technologies, a producer of communications equipment, begins his "Letter to Shareholders" in 2000 with, "This was a tough year for Lucent Technologies." That seems honest enough, with Lucent's earnings down 75 percent. He admits that the company had issues of "execution and focus." But

after discussing the problems, he goes on to say, "In many ways, I view this as a rebirth of Lucent." The *rebirth* turned out to be a *$4.7 billion loss* in fiscal 2001.

2. In the 1997 Sunbeam® report, the letter to shareholders from Chairman and CEO Albert Dunlap begins, "We had an amazing year in 1997! During the past 12 months we set new records in almost every facet of the Company's operations. . . . By July 1997, the Company had completed the major initiatives to transform the Company into a leaner, more profitable company, positioned to sustain strong revenue growth through the introduction of new products and expanded distribution." Whoa. In this so-called "amazing year," Sunbeam failed to generate any cash from its business operations, posting a negative $8.2 billion in operating cash flow. The 1997 annual report numbers, as well as those in preceding and succeeding years, had to be restated because improper recognition of revenue resulted in an overstatement of the 1997 profits. (Much more discussion of revenue recognition is provided in Chapter 2.) Sunbeam went much further downhill from there, ultimately filing for bankruptcy protection in 2001.

The most important information in a corporate annual report is the basic set of financial statements: statement of earnings (income statement), statement of financial condition (balance sheet), statement of shareholders' equity, and statement of cash flows. These statements are presented here (Exhibits 1-1, 1-2, 1-3, 1-4) for Eastman Kodak Company, and each will be discussed and explained in detail in Chapters 2 through 4, then analyzed in Chapter 5. The entire section of notes is not included here, but those notes relevant to particular items on the financial statements and to the analysis are shown and discussed in related sections.

Exhibit 1-1
Eastman Kodak Company and Subsidiary Companies
Consolidated Statement of Earnings

For the Year Ended December 31, (in millions, except per share data)	2000	1999	1998
Sales	$ 13,994	$ 14,089	$ 13,406
Cost of goods sold	8,019	7,987	7,293
Gross profit	5,975	6,102	6,113
Selling, general and administrative expenses	2,977	3,295	3,303
Research and development costs	784	817	922
Earnings from operations	2,214	1,990	1,888
Interest expense	178	142	110
Other income (charges)	96	261	328
Earnings before income taxes	2,132	2,109	2,106
Provision for income taxes	725	717	716
Net earnings	$ 1,407	$ 1,392	$ 1,390
Basic earnings per share	$ 4.62	$ 4.38	$ 4.30
Diluted earnings per share	$ 4.59	$ 4.33	$ 4.24
Earnings used in basic and diluted earnings per share	$ 1,407	$ 1,392	$ 1,390
Number of common shares used in basic earnings per share	304.9	318.0	323.3
Incremental shares from assumed conversion of options	1.7	3.5	4.5
Number of common shares used in diluted earnings per share	306.6	321.5	327.8

The accompanying notes are an integral part of these financial statements.

Exhibit 1-2
Eastman Kodak Company and Subsidiary Companies
Consolidated Statement of Financial Position

At December 31, (in millions, except share and per share data)	2000	1999
Assets		
Current Assets		
Cash and cash equivalents	$ 246	$ 373
Marketable securities	5	20
Receivables	2,653	2,537
Inventories	1,718	1,519
Deferred income tax charges	575	689
Other	294	306
Total current assets	5,491	5,444
Properties		
Land, buildings and equipment at cost	12,963	13,289
Less: Accumulated depreciation	7,044	7,342
Net properties	5,919	5,947
Other Assets		
Goodwill (net of accumulated amortization of $778 and $671)	947	982
Long-term receivables and other noncurrent assets	1,767	1,801
Deferred income tax charges	88	196
Total Assets	$ 14,212	$ 14,370
Liabilities and Shareholders' Equity		
Current Liabilities		
Payables	$ 3,275	$ 3,832
Short-term borrowings	2,206	1,163
Taxes — income and other	572	612
Dividends payable	128	139
Deferred income tax credits	34	23
Total current liabilities	6,215	5,769
Other Liabilities		
Long-term borrowings	1,166	936
Postemployment liabilities	2,610	2,776
Other long-term liabilities	732	918
Deferred income tax credits	61	59
Total Liabilities	10,784	10,458
Shareholders' Equity		
Common stock, par value $2.50 per share 950,000,000 shares authorized;		
issued 391,292,760 shares in 2000 and 1999	978	978
Additional paid in capital	871	889
Retained earnings	7,869	6,995
Accumulated other comprehensive loss	(482)	(145)
	9,236	8,717
Treasury stock, at cost 100,808,494 shares in 2000 and 80,871,830 shares in 1999	5,808	4,805
Total Shareholders' Equity	3,428	3,912
Total Liabilities and Shareholders' Equity	$ 14,212	$ 14,370

The accompanying notes are an integral part of these financial statements.

Exhibit 1-3
Eastman Kodak Company and Subsidiary Companies
Consolidated Statement of Shareholders' Equity

(in millions, except number of shares)	Common Stock*	Additional Paid In Capital	Retained Earnings	Accumulated Other Comprehensive Income(Loss)	Treasury Stock	Total
Shareholders' Equity December 31, 1997	$ 978	$ 914	$ 5,343	$ (202)	$ (3,872)	$ 3,161
Net earnings	–	–	1,390	–	–	1,390
Other comprehensive income (loss):						
Unrealized holding gains arising during the period						
($122 million pre-tax)	–	–	–	–	–	80
Reclassification adjustment for gains included in net earnings						
($66 million pre-tax)	–	–	–	–	–	(44)
Currency translation adjustments	–	–	–	–	–	59
Minimum pension liability adjustment ($7 million pre-tax)	–	–	–	–	–	(4)
Other comprehensive income	–	–	–	91	–	91
Comprehensive income	–	–	–	–	–	1,481
Cash dividends declared	–	–	(570)	–	–	(570)
Treasury stock repurchased (3,541,295 shares)	–	–	–	–	(258)	(258)
Treasury stock issued under employee plans (3,272,713 shares)	–	(58)	–	–	186	128
Tax reductions — employee plans	–	46	–	–	–	46
Shareholders' Equity December 31, 1998	978	902	6,163	(111)	(3,944)	3,988
Net earnings	–	–	1,392	–	–	1,392
Other comprehensive income (loss):						
Unrealized holding gains arising during the period						
($115 million pre-tax)	–	–	–	–	–	83
Reclassification adjustment for gains included in net earnings						
($20 million pre-tax)	–	–	–	–	–	(13)
Currency translation adjustments	–	–	–	–	–	(118)
Minimum pension liability adjustment ($26 million pre-tax)	–	–	–	–	–	14
Other comprehensive loss	–	–	–	(34)	–	(34)
Comprehensive income	–	–	–	–	–	1,358
Cash dividends declared	–	–	(560)	–	–	(560)
Treasury stock repurchased (13,482,648 shares)	–	–	–	–	(925)	(925)
Treasury stock issued under employee plans (1,105,220 shares)	–	(24)	–	–	64	40
Tax reductions — employee plans	–	11	–	–	–	11
Shareholders' Equity December 31, 1999	978	889	6,995	(145)	(4,805)	3,912
Net earnings	–	–	1,407	–	–	1,407
Other comprehensive income (loss):						
Unrealized holding loss arising during the period						
($77 million pre-tax)	–	–	–	–	–	(48)
Reclassification adjustment for gains included in net earnings						
($94 million pre-tax)	–	–	–	–	–	(58)
Unrealized loss arising from hedging activity ($55 million pre-tax)	–	–	–	–	–	(34)
Reclassification adjustment for hedging related gains						
included in net earnings ($6 million pre-tax)	–	–	–	–	–	(4)
Currency translation adjustments	–	–	–	–	–	(194)
Minimum pension liability adjustment ($2 million pre-tax)	–	–	–	–	–	1
Other comprehensive loss	–	–	–	(337)	–	(337)
Comprehensive income	–	–	–	–	–	1,070
Cash dividends declared	–	–	(533)	–	–	(533)
Treasury stock repurchased (21,575,536 shares)	–	–	–	–	(1,099)	(1,099)
Treasury stock issued under employee plans (1,638,872 shares)	–	(33)	–	–	96	63
Tax reductions — employee plans	–	15	–	–	–	15
Shareholders' Equity December 31, 2000	$ 978	$ 871	$ 7,869	$ (482)	$ (5,808)	$ 3,428

*There are 100 million shares of $10 par value preferred stock authorized, none of which have been issued.

Accumulated unrealized holding gains, related to available for sale securities, as of December 31, 2000, 1999 and 1998 were $7 million, $113 million, and $43 million, respectively. Accumulated unrealized losses related to hedging activity as of December 31, 2000 were $(38). Accumulated translation adjustments as of December 31, 2000, 1999 and 1998 were $(425) million, $(231) million and $(113) million, respectively. Accumulated minimum pension liability adjustments as of December 31, 2000, 1999 and 1998 were $(26) million, $(27) million and $(41) million, respectively.

The accompanying notes are an integral part of these financial statements.

Exhibit 1-4
Eastman Kodak Company and Subsidiary Companies
Consolidated Statement of Cash Flows

For the Year Ended December 31, (in millions)	2000	1999	1998
Cash flows from operating activities:			
Net earnings	$ 1,407	$ 1,392	$ 1,390
Adjustments to reconcile to net cash provided by operating activities:			
Depreciation and amortization	889	918	853
Gains on sales of businesses/assets	(117)	(162)	(166)
Restructuring costs, asset impairments and other charges	–	453	42
Provision for deferred income taxes	235	247	202
Increase in receivables	(247)	(121)	(1)
Increase in inventories	(282)	(201)	(43)
Decrease in liabilities excluding borrowings	(755)	(478)	(516)
Other items, net	(148)	(115)	(278)
Total adjustments	(425)	541	93
Net cash provided by operating activities	982	1,933	1,483
Cash flows from investing activities:			
Additions to properties	(945)	(1,127)	(1,108)
Proceeds from sales of businesses/assets	276	468	297
Cash flows related to sales of businesses	1	(46)	(59)
Acquisitions, net of cash acquired	(130)	(3)	(949)
Marketable securities — sales	84	127	162
Marketable securities — purchases	(69)	(104)	(182)
Net cash used in investing activities	(783)	(685)	(1,839)
Cash flows from financing activities:			
Net increase (decrease) in borrowings with original maturities of 90 days or less	939	(136)	894
Proceeds from other borrowings	1,310	1,343	1,133
Repayment of other borrowings	(936)	(1,118)	(1,251)
Dividends to shareholders	(545)	(563)	(569)
Exercise of employee stock options	43	44	128
Stock repurchase programs	(1,125)	(897)	(258)
Net cash (used in) provided by financing activities	(314)	(1,327)	77
Effect of exchange rate changes on cash	(12)	(5)	8
Net decrease in cash and cash equivalents	(127)	(84)	(271)
Cash and cash equivalents, beginning of year	373	457	728
Cash and cash equivalents, end of year	$ 246	$ 373	$ 457
Supplemental Cash Flow Information			
Cash paid for interest and income taxes was:			
Interest, net of portion capitalized of $40, $36 and $41	$ 166	$ 120	$ 90
Income taxes	486	445	498
The following transactions are not reflected in the Consolidated Statement of Cash Flows:			
Contribution of assets to Kodak Polychrome Graphics joint venture	$ –	$ 13	$ –
Minimum pension liability adjustment	(1)	(14)	4
Liabilities assumed in acquisitions	31	–	473

The accompanying notes are an integral part of these financial statements.

Financial Statements

The **consolidated statement of earnings** (or income statement) shows the results of a firm's operations, breaking down the components of revenue and expense; other sources of income and expense; net profit or loss; and net profit or loss per share for an accounting period (Chapter 2).

The **consolidated statement of financial position** (or balance sheet) presents assets, liabilities, and shareholders' equity—what the firm owns and what it owes to creditors and owners—at a particular date, such as the end of the year or the quarter (Chapter 3).

The **consolidated statement of shareholders' equity** reconciles the beginning and ending balances of all the accounts that appear in the shareholders' equity section of the statement of financial condition (Chapter 3).

The **statement of cash flows** provides information about inflows and outflows of cash—where the cash comes from and where it goes during an accounting period—segregated by operating, financing, and investing activities (Chapter 4).

Notes to the Financial Statements

The material that immediately follows the presentation of the four financial statements is a section of notes to the financial statements. The notes are an integral part of the statements and must be consulted in order to understand and evaluate some of the material on the face of each financial statement. The first note is a summary of the firm's accounting policies. Other notes present details about specific accounts and financial matters. The notes for Eastman Kodak Company are as follows:

Note 1: Significant Accounting Policies
Note 2: Receivables
Note 3: Inventories
Note 4: Properties
Note 5: Payables and Short-Term Borrowings
Note 6: Long-Term Borrowings
Note 7: Other Long-Term Liabilities
Note 8: Commitments and Contingencies
Note 9: Financial Instruments
Note 10: Income Taxes
Note 11: Restructuring Programs and Cost Reduction
Note 12: Retirement Plans
Note 13: Nonpension Postretirement Benefits
Note 14: Stock Option and Compensation Plans
Note 15: Acquisitions and Joint Ventures
Note 16: Sales of Assets and Divestitures
Note 17: Segment Information
Note 18: Subsequent Events
Note 19: Quarterly Sales and Earnings Data—Unaudited

Financial statements and their accompanying notes contain a wealth of useful information regarding the success of a company's operating performance, its financial condition and structure, the ability of the firm to generate needed cash from its operations, the policies and strategies of management, and insight into the firm's future prospects. Getting to what matters for an individual user may be difficult because of the complexity and volume of information presented as well as the leeway accorded management in choices of accounting policies and the discretion involved in applying those policies. The objective of these chapters is to help readers of annual reports find what is needed and interpret the information in a way that is helpful to the user's specific needs.

Report of Independent Auditors

Management is responsible for the preparation of financial statements, and annual reports contain a letter explaining this responsibility. The job of the independent accountants is to audit the financial statements and attest to the fairness of their presentation. The result of this objective, outside audit is presented in an independent auditors' report.

An **unqualified** report states that the financial statements present fairly, in all material respects, the financial position of the company, the results of operations, and the cash flows, in conformity with generally accepted accounting principles. The "Report of Independent Accountants" from the 2000 Annual Report for Eastman Kodak Company is shown in Exhibit 1-5.

Some situations result in an **unqualified opinion with explanatory language**—such as a consistency departure due to a change in accounting principles; uncertainties caused by future events such as contract disputes and lawsuits; or events that the auditors wish to describe because they may present business risk or issues affecting

Exhibit 1-5
Eastman Kodak Company Report of Independent Accountants

To the Board,

In our opinion, the accompanying consolidated financial statements appearing on pages 43 through 63 of this Annual Report present fairly, in all material respects, the financial position of Eastman Kodak Company and subsidiary companies (Kodak) at December 31, 2000 and 1999, and the results of operations and their cash flows for each of the three years in the period ended December 31, 2000, in conformity with generally accepted accounting principles in the United States of America. These financial statements are the responsibility of the Company's management; our responsibility is to express an opinion on these financial statements based on our audits. We conducted our audits of these statements in accordance with auditing standards generally accepted in the United States of America, which require that we plan and perform the audit to obtain reasonable assurance about whether the financial statements are free of material misstatement. An audit includes examining, on a test basis, evidence supporting the amounts and disclosures in the financial statements, assessing the accounting principles used and significant estimates made by management, and evaluating the overall financial statement presentation. We believe that our audits provide a reasonable basis for the opinion expressed above.

Pricewaterhouse Coopers LLP
Rochester, New York
January 15, 2001

Exhibit 1-6

Exerpt from Chiquita Brands International, Inc. 2000 Audit Report

The accompanying financial statements have been prepared assuming that Chiquita Brands International, Inc. will continue as a going concern. The Company announced an initiative on January 16, 2001 to restructure publicly held debt issued by Chiquita Brands International, Inc., the parent holding company. In connection with this restructuring initiative, the Company suspended all principal and interest payments on this debt, including the January 2001 interest payment on the 9 5/8% senior notes due 2004. The failure to make this interest payment constitutes an event of default that permits the holders of such notes to accelerate their maturity. These conditions raise substantial doubt about the Company's ability to continue as a going concern. These matters and management's plans are more fully discussed in Note 2 to the financial statements. The financial statements do not include any adjustments that might result from the outcome of this uncertainty.

whether the firm will continue to operate. These reports result in an additional paragraph such as the audit report shown in Exhibit 1-6 from Ernst & Young for the 2000 Chiquita® Brands International Inc. Annual Report.

Some circumstances, such as a departure from generally accepted accounting principles or a scope limitation, warrant a **qualified** auditors' report. For example, the departure from GAAP would result in the following language in the opinion sentence: "In our opinion, except for the (nature of the departure explained), the financial statements present fairly. . . ." If the departure affects numerous accounts and financial statement relationships, an **adverse opinion** is rendered. A scope limitation means the extent of the work has been limited, and this will result in a qualified opinion unless the limitation is so material as to require a **disclaimer of opinion,** which means the auditor cannot evaluate the fairness of the statements.

Accounting Trends and Techniques is an annual document published by the American Institute of Certified Public Accountants reviewing the financial statement presentations of 600 companies. In the 2001 volume, which shows the results from the year 2000 annual reports, 19 companies had unqualified opinions with explanatory language related to uncertainties; 69 had unqualified opinions with explanatory language because of a lack of consistency; and none of the 600 companies contained a qualified opinion.[9]

Any change in the firm's outside auditor may be a signal of internal problems and disagreements over disclosures. Firms that change auditors are required to file Form 8-K with the SEC. In 1999, Rite Aid's auditing firm, KPMG, resigned saying they were unable to rely on management's representations. Subsequently, Rite Aid reported a $1.1 billion loss for fiscal 2000 and restated earnings for 1999 and 1998, turning previously reported earnings to large losses.

In theory, the auditing firm performing the audit and issuing the report is "independent" of the firm being audited. The annual report reader should be aware, however, that the auditor is hired by the firm whose financial statements are under review. Although some of these practices may change as a result of congressional hearings following the Enron collapse, the same auditing firms frequently do consulting, tax, and

---

[9] Andy Mrakovcic (Ed.), *Accounting Trends and Techniques* (New York: American Institute of Certified Public Accountants, 2001), pp. 584, 587, 597.

other highly lucrative work for the same firm. Many firms hire accountants from their auditing firms to prepare the financial statements and serve in other top-level financial positions. The potential for conflict of interest is ever present in this situation in which the outside auditor must satisfy the client. In recent years, the financial press has been rife with reports of cases filed and penalties levied against auditing firms. Auditors have paid heavily for suits involving W. R. Grace & Company (Price Waterhouse), Cendant Corporation (Ernst & Young), and Sunbeam Corporation (Arthur Andersen).

In 2001, the SEC brought civil fraud charges against the accounting firm, Arthur Andersen, which agreed to pay a $7 million penalty, the largest ever for an accounting firm, for its failure in the audit of Waste Management Inc.® that ultimately led to a $1.4 billion restatement of earnings in 1998. Waste Management had overstated profits in the early- and mid-1990s with Andersen giving clean audit reports throughout the period. All of Waste Management's top financial officials were former Andersen auditors.[10]

At Styling Technology Corporation, a maker of beauty products in Arizona, a division manager expected questions from auditors about $4 million in bogus sales of sun-tanning products recorded during the final week of 1998 when, in fact, the company typically did almost all of its volume in the first half of the year. Arthur Andersen gave a clean report, and the fraud was not detected until the division manager reported it to the SEC. Styling Technology bondholders filing suit alleged that the accounting firm's independence was compromised because the company paid Andersen $7.5 million and hired eight Andersen auditors and consultants for financial positions within the firm.[11]

The Enron case has highlighted the relationship many companies have with the accounting firms that audit the financial reports while also serving as financial consultants, to the tune of millions of dollars each year. In 2000, Enron paid Andersen fees of $52 million, $25 million for auditing and the remainder for other work, including consulting.[12]

In 1999 the SEC released a study of registrants alleged to be involved in fraudulent financial reporting. External auditors were named in 29 percent of the cases either for being involved in the fraud or for negligent auditing; in 25 percent of the cases, companies had changed auditors prior to the fraudulent reporting period.[13] Given the rash of lawsuits and penalties against accounting firms and the many highly publicized business failures, the SEC and AICPA have attempted to tighten rules in an effort to minimize fraud. During his tenure, former SEC chief Arthur Levitt offered recommendations on how the SEC can tighten regulatory oversight,[14] and he reiterated his suggestions in congressional hearings on Enron. Lynn Turner, former accounting enforcement chief at the SEC and now Director of the Center for Quality Financial Reporting at Colorado State University, remains a strident critic of the accounting industry. He believes the accounting problems reflect the fact that the

---

[10] Floyd Norris, "Big Five Accounting Firm To Pay Fine in Fraud Case," *The New York Times* (June 20, 2001), p. 1.

[11] David Dietz, "Insider accuses Andersen of fraud," *The Arizona Republic* (January 14, 2002), pp. D1, D4.

[12] Jonathan Weil, "What Enron's Financial Reports Did—and Didn't—Reveal," *The Wall Street Journal* (November 5, 2001), pp. C1, C14.

[13] Mark S. Beasley, Joseph V. Carcello, and Dana R. Hermanson, "COSO's New Fraud Study: What It Means for CPA's," *Journal of Accountancy* (May 1999) pp. 12–13.

[14] "Arthur Levitt Addresses 'Illusions,' " *Journal of Accountancy* (December 1998), pp. 12–13.

public's needs have been ignored.[15] The current SEC chair Harvey Pitt has proposed an independent oversight group to oversee audits. The process now in place involves peer review, one auditing firm checking up on another.

Management Discussion and Analysis

The Management Discussion and Analysis (MD&A) section can be a valuable tool in evaluating a company because it contains insight into the firm's own perspective on its performance, and this section also presents qualitative information that cannot be found in the financial data. The MD&A includes coverage of any favorable or unfavorable trends and significant events or uncertainties in the categories of liquidity, capital resources, and results of operations. ‚

In the 2000 Annual Report of Eastman Kodak Company, the MD&A section begins with a discussion of the years 2000, 1999, and 1998—and a comparison of 2000 with 1999, and 1999 with 1998. Other topics covered are the firm's restructuring programs, outlook, effect of the Euro (the single European currency), liquidity and capital resources, a cautionary statement about the company's forward-looking statements, market price data, and quantitative and qualitative disclosures about market risk. Material in this section is utilized in the coverage and analysis of Eastman Kodak's financial statements in Chapters 2–5.

Although the MD&A section is useful to the annual report reader, there are also limits to the value of this material because, again, it is management's "take" on the company situation. One of the goals of the SEC in mandating the inclusion and content of this material was to make publicly available information about future events and trends that might affect future performance. One study[16] to determine the effectiveness of the MD&A section concluded that companies did a good job of describing the past but did little to predict the future. Many companies essentially provided no forward-looking information at all. In the past, the SEC has taken action if a company fails to disclose key information. For example, Caterpillar® Inc. omitted from its MD&A the fact that a fourth of its 1989 income, from a Brazilian unit, would be nonrecurring. An SEC spokesperson characterized the action against Caterpillar as a message that the SEC takes the guidelines for disclosures in the MD&A section seriously.[17]

Five-Year Summary and Market Data

The 5-year summary of key performance measures provides an overview of the firm's performance and financial condition in some major categories. Full financial statements, however, are required to perform an analysis of the company. Many key items, such as cash flow from operations, do not appear in the summary.

---

[15] David Milstead, "Ex-SEC watchdog saw writing on the wall," *Rocky Mountain News* (February 2, 2002), pp. 1C, 12C.

[16] Moses L. Parva and Marc J. Epstein, "How Good Is MD&A as an Investment Tool?" *Journal of Accountancy* (March 1993), pp. 51–53.

[17] "A Disciplinary Message from the SEC," *Journal of Accountancy* (March 1993), p. 53.

Exhibit 1-7
Eastman Kodak Company and Subsidiary Companies
Summary of Operating Data

(Dollar amounts and shares in millions, except per share data)	2000	1999	1998	1997	1996
Sales from continuing operations	$ 13,994	$ 14,089	$ 13,406	$ 14,538	$ 15,968
Earnings from operations	2,214	1,990	1,888	130	1,845
Earnings from continuing operations after tax	1,407[1]	1,392[2]	1,390[8]	5[5]	1,011[7]
Earnings from discontinued operations after tax	–	–	–	–	277
Net earnings	1,407[1]	1,392[2]	1,390[9]	5[5]	1,288[7]
Earnings and Dividends					
Net earnings					
— % of sales	10.1%	9.9%	10.4%	0.0%	8.1%
— % return on average shareholders' equity	38.3%	35.2%	38.9%	0.1%	26.1%
Basic earnings per share	4.62	4.38	4.30	.01	3.82[8]
Diluted earnings per share	4.59	4.33	4.24	.01	3.76[8]
Cash dividends declared					
— on common shares	533	560	570	577	539
— per common share	1.76	1.76	1.76	1.76	1.60
Common shares outstanding at year end	290.5	310.4	322.8	323.1	331.8
Shareholders at year end	113,308	131,719	129,495	135,132	137,092
Statement of Financial Position Data					
Working capital[9]	$ 1,482	$ 838	$ 939	$ 909	$ 2,089
Properties — net	5,919	5,947	5,914	5,509	5,422
Total assets	14,212	14,370	14,733	13,145	14,438
Short-term borrowings	2,206	1,163	1,518	611	541
Long-term borrowings	1,166	936	504	585	559
Total shareholders' equity	3,428	3,912	3,988	3,161	4,734
Supplemental Information					
Sales — Consumer Imaging	$ 7,406	$ 7,411	$ 7,164	$ 7,681	$ 7,659
— Kodak Professional	1,706	1,910	1,840	2,272	2,367
— Health Imaging	2,185	2,120	1,526	1,532	1,627
— Other Imaging	2,697	2,648	2,876	3,053	4,315
Research and development costs	784	817	922[4]	1,230[6]	1,028
Depreciation	738	773	737	748	837
Taxes (excludes payroll, sales and excise taxes)	933	806	809	164	663
Wages, salaries and employee benefits	3,726	3,962	4,306	4,985	5,110
Employees at year end					
— in the U.S.	43,200	43,300	46,300	54,800	53,400
— worldwide	78,400	80,650	86,200	97,500	94,800

(1) Includes charges related to the sale and exit of a manufacturing facility of $50 million, which reduced net earnings by $39 million.
(2) Includes $350 million of restructuring charges, which reduced net earnings by $231 million, and an additional $11 million of charges related to this restructuring program, which reduced net earnings by $7 million; $103 million of charges associated with business exits, which reduced net earnings by $68 million; a gain of $95 million on the sale of The Image Bank, which increased net earnings by $63 million; and a gain of $25 million on the sale of the Motion Analysis Systems Division, which increased net earnings by $16 million.
(3) Includes $35 million of litigation charges, which reduced net earnings by $23 million; $132 million of Office Imaging charges, which reduced net earnings by $87 million; $45 million primarily for a write-off of in-process R&D associated with the Imation acquisition, which reduced net earnings by $30 million; a gain of $87 million on the sale of NanoSystems, which increased net earnings by $57 million; and a gain of $66 million on the sale of part of the Company's investment in Gretag, which increased net earnings by $44 million.
(4) Includes a $42 million charge for the write-off of in-process R&D associated with the Imation acquisition.
(5) Includes $1,455 million of restructuring costs, asset impairments and other charges, which reduced net earnings by $990 million; $186 million for a write-off of in-process R&D associated with the Wang acquisition, which reduced net earnings by $123 million; and a $46 million litigation charge, which reduced net earnings by $30 million.
(6) Includes a $186 million charge for the write-off of in-process R&D associated with the Wang acquisition.
(7) Includes $358 million of restructuring costs, which reduced net earnings by $256 million, and a $387 million loss related to the sale of the Office Imaging business, which reduced net earnings by $252 million.
(8) Basic and diluted earnings per share from continuing operations were $3.00 and $2.95, respectively.
(9) Excludes short-term borrowings.

One of the noteworthy features of Eastman Kodak's Summary (shown in Exhibit 1-7) is the number of footnotes required to explain the numbers. The items in the notes—restructuring charges, asset sales, litigation charges, asset write-offs—have had a major impact on the firm's earnings and are discussed in Chapter 2.

The market price data gives a snapshot of the common stock performance over a 2-year period, showing the high and low price for each quarter. This information for Kodak is as follows:

	2000		1999	
Price per share:	High	Low	High	Low
First Quarter	$67.50	$53.31	$80.38	$62.31
Second Quarter	63.63	53.19	79.81	60.81
Third Quarter	65.69	39.75	78.25	68.25
Fourth Quarter	48.50	35.31	77.50	56.63

Source: Eastman Kodak Annual Report 2000.

This downward trend in Kodak's share price is one of the areas of focus for the analysis of the company in Chapter 5.

A PERSONAL STORY

An example, based on the following true story, is used to illustrate how the content of this book can be effectively used. After completing her undergraduate degree, Eleanor Fraser, the daughter of one of the book's authors, was employed by Enron Corporation in 1997. Among the decisions Eleanor faced at the outset of her employment were questions regarding her pension plan, including whether or not to put a portion of her 401(k) contribution into Enron's common stock; the company's portion was automatically invested in the company's stock.

To help her daughter make the investment decision, Lyn sat down with Eleanor at the kitchen table to review what is now probably a collector's item: the "1996 Enron Annual Report to Shareholders and Customers." After flipping through the slick pages with a colored picture of Chairman Kenneth L. Lay and President Jeffrey K. Skilling, the lovely bar charts showing rising trends in earnings and dividends, the glossy photos of persons benefiting from Enron's work, and the sidebar graphs documenting Enron's successes, Lyn turned to the plain paper section of the report with the financial statements and notes. What Lyn saw that eventually led her to recommend that Eleanor *not* invest in Enron stock related to the company's (1) revenue growth relative to earnings, (2) bad debt provisions, (3) cash flow from operations, and (4) off-balance-sheet activities. (All of these topics are explored and explained with more detail later in the book.)

Revenue Versus Operating Earnings

Enron's Consolidated Income Statement reports the following revenues and earnings for the 3 years presented in the 1996 annual report:

(in millions)	1996	1995	1994
Total revenues	$13,289	9,189	8,984
Operating income	690	618	716
Net income	584	520	453

Source: 1996 Enron Annual Report.

Revenues are increasing over the period—by 48 percent between 1994 and 1996—but operating income has actually declined, and net income has grown 29 percent, a much slower pace than revenues. This combination signals at least a caution flag because the company may be growing too fast, costs may be out of line, or revenue recognition may be overly aggressive.

Accounts Receivable Relative to the Allowance for Doubtful Accounts

Supporting the growth in revenues, it is not surprising to find a big increase in receivables, the amounts Enron's customers owe from purchases on credit; but one would also expect at least a comparable increase in the amounts Enron is allowing for debts that will not be paid, called the "allowance for doubtful accounts." Instead, Enron's balance sheet (balance sheets show only 2 years) reflects for the 2 years presented a 65 percent *increase* in receivables but a 50 percent *decrease* in the allowance account:

(in millions)	1996	1995
Trade receivables (net of allowance for doubtful accounts of $6 and $12)	$1,841	1,116

Source: 1996 Enron Annual Report.

Again, this could indicate a problem because the company may be overstating earnings by not making adequate provision for prospective bad debts.

Cash Flow

One of the points that is hammered home in this book is the importance of operating cash flow as a performance measure, and a caution flag is warranted when net income and cash flow from operations are moving in different directions, or when net income is growing faster than cash flow. Enron's earnings grew smoothly and steadily between 1994 and 1996, which certainly looks good on the surface to current and prospective investors:

(in millions)	1996	1995	1994
Net Income	$ 584	520	453

Source: 1996 Enron Annual Report.

But the generation of cash flow from operations shows something else entirely, a roller coaster with no cash generated by operations in 1995:

(in millions)	1996	1995	1994
Net Cash Provided by (Used in) Operating Activities	$1,040	(15)	460

Source: 1996 Enron Annual Report.

What a company needs—in order to compensate its employees, to service debt, to pay dividends to shareholders, and to grow—is success in generating cash from its business operations. Net income and cash flow are not the same because net income is measured by the accrual basis of accounting (explained fully in Chapter 2) rather than by the cash basis of accounting. The statement of cash flows (Chapter 4) shows the adjustments of net income used to calculate cash flow from operations, and it also shows sources and uses of cash from financing and investing activities. For example, this information reveals that Enron's negative cash from operations in 1995 required the company to borrow heavily to service debt and pay dividends, even though the company reported profits.

Although the gyration of cash from operations experienced by Enron in 1994–1996 does not necessarily indicate trouble, it does, at a minimum, suggest the need for additional analysis to understand the discrepancy between earnings and operating cash flow. From reading the notes and evaluating relevant accounts, it was difficult to accept with total confidence Enron's ability to sustain the turnaround in operating cash flow during 1996, in part because of the complexity and uncertainties relating to Enron's trading activities. The cash flow statement from Eleanor's annual report still bears a spot of spilled coffee to document the ladies' research.

Enron Corp. and Subsidiaries

Consolidated Statement of Cash Flows

(In Millions)	Year Ended December 31,		
	1996	1995	1994
Cash Flows From Operating Activities			
Reconciliation of net income to net cash provided by (used in) operating activities			
Net income	$ 584	$ 520	$ 453
Depreciation, depletion and amortization	474	432	441
Oil and gas exploration expenses	89	70	84
Deferred income taxes	207	216	93
Gains on sales of assets	(274)	(530)	(91)
Regulatory, litigation and other contingency adjustments	23	112	(25)
Changes in components of working capital	142	(834)	(142)
Net assets from price risk management activities	15	(98)	(165)
Amortization of production payment transaction	(43)	(43)	(43)
Other, net	(177)	131	(157)
Net Cash Provided by (Used in) Operating Activities	1,040	(15)	460
Cash Flows From Investing Activities			
Proceeds from sales of investments and other assets	477	906	440
Additions to property, plant and equipment	(855)	(731)	(661)
Equity investments	(761)	(170)	(272)
Other, net	(91)	(82)	(67)
Net Cash Provided by (Used in) Investing Activities	(1,230)	13	(560)
Cash Flows From Financing Activities			
Net increase (decrease) in short-term borrowings	217	(250)	115
Issuance of long-term debt	359	907	190
Repayment of long-term debt	(290)	(448)	(162)
Issuance of company-obligated preferred stock of subsidiaries	215	—	165
Issuance of common stock	102	20	67
Dividends paid	(281)	(254)	(231)
Net acquisition (disposition) of treasury stock	5	(64)	(41)
Other, net	8	14	(9)
Net Cash Provided by (Used in) Financing Activities	331	(15)	92
Increase (Decrease) in Cash and Cash Equivalents	141	(17)	(8)
Cash and Cash Equivalents, Beginning of Year	115	132	140
Cash and Cash Equivalents, End of Year	$ 256	$ 115	$ 132
Changes in Components of Working Capital			
Receivables	$ (678)	$ (639)	$ (280)
Inventories	(53)	27	(25)
Payables	870	126	(82)
Accrued taxes	(51)	30	12
Accrued interest	4	(7)	5
Other	50	(371)	208
Total	$ 142	$ (834)	$ (142)

The accompanying notes are an integral part of these consolidated financial statements.

Consolidated Statement of Cash Flows from 1996 Enron Annual Report with spilled coffee.

Items Not on the Balance Sheet

On Enron's Consolidated Balance Sheet, between the liabilities and equity sections, there is a line that reads, "Commitments and Contingencies (Notes 2, 3, 8, 13, 14 and 15)."

These particular notes include extensive discussions of financial information that is relevant to the company's current and future operations but that is not required to be quantified on the balance sheet. These are permissible accounting practices relating to such items for Enron as a proposed merger, price risk management and financial instruments, unconsolidated subsidiaries, regulatory issues, and litigation. But the sheer number and volume of these items signaled not that anything was necessarily wrong but that there were more caution flags. In fact, by 2001 these flags turned out to be very red indeed!

Enron's 1996 Annual Report contains an unqualified report from its independent auditors, and there was nothing to suggest that anything was seriously amiss. In fact, Enron appeared to have 3 strong years of impressive performance and a rising stock price after this report was issued. What the evaluation of Enron's report suggested was that the company might be growing too fast for its own underpinnings and that there was a hint of "smoke and mirrors" when an effort was made to find answers to specific questions about such items as the accounts underlying the gyration of cash flow. The ultimate downfall of Enron was much more complicated than the hints found here, and many of the problems developed from activities subsequent to this annual report. But the wariness that resulted from the pieces of analysis previously described resulted in the recommendation that Eleanor go elsewhere with her portion of the 401(k) funds, which she did: a *rare case* in which Eleanor admits to following her mother's advice. As a result, she still has the bulk of those funds intact. The issues raised in the evaluation of Enron's annual report are ones that are explained in more detail in relevant sections of this book as part of the process involved in reading and interpreting any corporate annual report.

Not all Wall Street analysts were fooled by Enron. One of the many other interesting "I told you so" stories to come out of the debacle is that of James Chanos,[18] a money manager at Kynikos Associates Ltd., a firm specializing in betting when a company's stock price will fall. One of the things Chanos correctly spotted by reading notes to the 1999 Enron annual report was the murkiness in Enron's off-balance-sheet partnerships. Chanos's research led to selling Enron's stock "short," which means selling borrowed shares and replacing them with cheaper shares when the price falls, which Enron's stock dramatically did. On a more humorous note, a reporter for *The Wall Street Journal* uncovered the key event foretelling of Enron's doom: paying big bucks to put its name on a baseball stadium in Houston—Enron Field. Enron joined Fruit of the Loom®, Trans World Airlines, PSINet® Inc., 3Com® Corporation, and several other companies in spiraling downward after attaching their names to a sports venue.[19]

READERS' CHECKLIST OF CAUTION FLAGS FROM CHAPTER 1

Several caution flags for users of annual reports have emerged from the topics discussed in Chapter 1. A preliminary list is provided here and will be expanded in subsequent chapters. Although the appearance of a caution flag does not

---

[18] Cassell Bryan-Low and Suzanee McGee, "Enron Short Seller Detected Red Flags in Regulatory Filings," *The Wall Street Journal* (November 5, 2001), pp. C1, C2.

[19] Scott Thurm, "Stadium Jinx: What to Call Enron Field? 'Enron Folds,' Maybe Firms That Put Their Names on Arenas Hit Hard Times; Former Trans World Dome," *The Wall Street Journal* (December 4, 2001), p. A1.

explain the problem or even confirm that a problem exists, it does signal the need to dig deeper.

➢ Change in auditors
➢ Departure from "unqualified" opinion in auditor's report with "exception or explanatory" language or qualification
➢ Charges filed by SEC against firm or auditors for issues relating to accounting and financial reporting
➢ Rising ratio of fluff to financial data

➢ Revenue and earnings growing at different rates or moving in opposite directions
➢ Allowance for doubtful accounts not keeping pace with accounts receivable
➢ Negative or erratic cash flow from operations
➢ Earnings and cash flow from operations moving at different rates or in opposite directions
➢ Numerous unquantified contingencies and commitments
➢ Company puts name on sports arena

TEST YOURSELF

Each chapter of this book concludes with a self-test that provides readers with an opportunity to assess their understanding of the material presented. Solutions are provided immediately following the Glossary at the end of the book.

1. Why should people making investment decisions be able to evaluate financial information for themselves?
    a. Relying on analysts' advice may not be helpful due to potential conflicts of interest between the companies recommended and the analysts.
    b. Currently there is skepticism about reliance on the independent auditor's report.
    c. Companies will no longer offer 401(k) plans.
    d. Both (a) and (b)
2. Which of the following statements is false?
    a. In the current environment, companies feel pressured to produce rising earnings.
    b. There have not been any cases or judgments against auditing firms.
    c. Companies find creative ways to confuse the public with financial reports.
    d. The Securities and Exchange Commission has alerted investors to treat analysts' advice with caution.
3. What is GAAP?
    a. A retail clothing chain
    b. An acronym for the principles used to prepare financial statements
    c. A regulatory body that works with Congress to oversee financial reporting
    d. The group of associated auditing practitioners that regulates auditing firms
4. Who is responsible for establishing accounting rules in the United States?
    a. The IASC and AICPA
    b. The SEC and IASC
    c. The SEC and FASB
    d. Auditors and analysts

5. What is a role of the Securities and Exchange Commission (SEC)?
   a. The SEC regulates companies that issue securities to the public.
   b. The SEC has statutory authority to set accounting and reporting standards.
   c. The SEC plays an oversight role in attempting to assure that companies' actual accounting practices follow stated principles.
   d. All of the above
6. How does a Form 10-K differ from an annual report mailed to shareholders?
   a. A form 10-K is the annual report required by the SEC and is usually more detailed than the annual report prepared primarily for shareholders and the general public.
   b. Form 10-Ks must be mailed to shareholders on a quarterly basis.
   c. A form 10-K is the annual report for private companies, whereas the annual report mailed to shareholders is for public companies.
   d. None of the above
7. What are the basic financial statements provided in an annual report?
   a. Statement of earnings and statement of cash flows
   b. Statement of financial condition and statement of earnings
   c. Statement of earnings, statement of financial condition, statement of shareholders' equity, and statement of cash flows
   d. Statement of earnings, statement of financial condition, statement of cash flows, and statement of market data
8. Which financial statement shows information about revenues, expenses, and net profit or loss?
   a. Statement of earnings
   b. Statement of financial condition
   c. Statement of shareholders' equity
   d. Statement of cash flows
9. Which financial statement shows information about assets, liabilities, and shareholders' equity?
   a. Statement of earnings
   b. Statement of financial condition
   c. Statement of shareholders' equity
   d. Statement of cash flows
10. Which financial statement provides information about inflows and outflows of cash?
    a. Statement of earnings
    b. Statement of financial condition
    c. Statement of shareholders' equity
    d. Statement of cash flows
11. Why are the notes to the financial statements important to read?
    a. The notes are needed to understand and evaluate some material on the face of each financial statement.
    b. The notes indicate whether the financial statements will be presented fairly.
    c. The notes must include information about future events and trends.
    d. Both (a) and (b)

12. What type of audit report states that the financial statements are presented fairly?
    a. A qualified auditors' report
    b. An adverse auditors' report
    c. An unqualified auditors' report
    d. A disclaimer of opinion
13. What is the purpose of the management discussion and analysis (MD&A)?
    a. The MD&A describes the accounting methods and policies used by the company to prepare the financial statements.
    b. The MD&A includes coverage of any favorable or unfavorable trends and significant events or uncertainties in the categories of liquidity, capital resources, and results of operations.
    c. The MD&A provides a 5-year summary of key performance measures and the market prices of the company's stock for a 2-year period.
    d. The MD&A contains all the "slick stuff," such as photos, the letter to the shareholders, and dazzling graphics.
14. What caused Lyn Fraser to advise her daughter Eleanor not to invest in Enron stock?
    a. Enron had just had the company's name attached to a sports venue.
    b. Enron appeared to have too much cash, but no profit.
    c. Revenue growth relative to earnings, provisions for doubtful accounts, cash flow from operations, and off-balance-sheet activities raised red flags.
    d. The spilled coffee on the Enron cash flow statement alerted Lyn to problems Enron was having with cash.

Chapter 2

Earnings—Real and Imagined

➤ *Why don't accounting rules prevent the problems?*

➤ *Statement of earnings—Kodak Company*

➤ *Profit measures, pro formas, and big baths*

➤ *Cooking the books*

➤ *Caution flags for users of annual reports*

➤ *Test yourself*

Company financial success has traditionally been measured by how much a firm earns in any given period. Investors, analysts, and creditors anxiously await each quarter's earnings report and compare the announced results with projections and expectations. At year-end, the focus is on a firm's bottom line—its profit for the year. Eastman Kodak Company (Kodak), for example, reported the following figures for net earnings and earnings per share in its 2000 annual report for the years ending December 31, 2000, 1999, and 1998:

	2000	1999	1998
Net earnings (in millions)	$1,407	1,392	1,390
Basic earnings per share	4.62	4.38	4.30

Source: Eastman Kodak Company Annual Report 2000.

Good job, Kodak. As the Chairman writes in his letter to shareholders, "... in the digital age, images drive value. And Kodak drives images." The company has reported steady increases in net earnings—the gains are not enormous, but profits are up and moving in the right direction. Earnings per share rose by 24 cents in 2000,

24

much better than the 8 cents in 1999. That's just what Kodak wants us to see and what we would expect from such a well-known and reputable company.

Unfortunately, the earnings numbers reported often bear little or no relationship to how well the company has actually performed. As dazzling as its annual report and reputation are, Kodak's reported figures may be misleading. That is something we explore in this chapter and the chapters that follow. Kodak Company's financial reports form the basis for the explanation and evaluation of each financial statement, and they contain lively fodder for discussion. But it is not the authors' intent to single out any one company for manipulating financial statement numbers. Kodak is among the hundreds of companies that show evidence of "earnings management," and examples of many other companies are included in the book. Some financial statements, like Kodak's, fall within the accounting rules, and others do not—resulting in SEC crackdowns, court cases, and required restatements.

The coverage of financial statements, in this and the following chapters, is intended to help readers get underneath the surface of the numbers and determine what's actually going on with a company rather than what the firm's management wants us to think. With the use of company examples and caution flags to supplement the in-depth look at financial statements, we hope to provide readers with the tools needed not only to understand and interpret the information presented, but also to spot potential problems. This chapter

- covers the earnings statement, beginning with a brief discussion of accounting rules and their relationship to earnings quality;
- takes readers step-by-step through Kodak's statement of earnings, featuring some of that company's creative accounting practices;
- discusses the merits (and demerits) of various measures of financial performance; and
- illustrates how some companies cook their books.

WHY DON'T ACCOUNTING RULES ENSURE QUALITY EARNINGS?

Understanding the earnings figures and other numbers in financial reports requires some knowledge of the accounting rules that underlie the presentation of financial statements. The approach taken in this book is to present only what is necessary—not to provide a full-blown course in accounting. Given the massive confusions generated by some companies' financial reporting, no amount of accounting would be enough to assure comprehension.

Basis of Accounting

Financial statements in the United States are prepared according to the **accrual basis of accounting.** Under accrual accounting, revenues (sales) are recorded when earned rather than when cash is received, and expenses (costs) are recorded when incurred rather than when the cash is paid out. Earnings are the difference between revenues and expenses for the period. Accrual accounting is based on the **matching principle,** which measures earnings by matching revenues against expenses for the accounting period in which they occur, regardless of cash inflow or outflow.

Translated, that means a firm records the revenue when the sale is made, even if the sale is made on credit and the customer doesn't pay until the next accounting period. If a company sells a 2-year service contract, the revenue is divided between the 2 years of the contract rather than recorded in the first year when the sale occurs and the cash is received. The same is true for expenses. If the company repairs equipment in December but doesn't pay the bill until January, the expense is still counted in December. Or, if a firm prepays 3 months' rent in November, 2 months' rent would be expensed this year and 1 month's next year. The idea is that expenses and revenues are allocated to the appropriate accounting period in determining profit for the period.

These examples to illustrate revenue and expense recognition, based on accrual accounting, are very simple and straightforward. But what if a company that manufactures barbecue grills wants to sell its products during the winter to customers like Wal-Mart® and Sears, that don't want to stock the items until the spring thaw? Let's say this company transfers the grills to a warehouse in December and pays to store them until March, when they are shipped out to the customers. When should the sale be recorded?

This is exactly the situation created by Sunbeam Corporation in the 1990s. Some companies use very liberal approaches, including fraudulent ones, in revenue and expense accounting. In an effort to boost revenues, Sunbeam chose to book the sales of backyard grills and related products during the winter months, even though the goods weren't shipped to customers until the spring. Sunbeam permitted customers to defer payment and also to return for full credit any unsold items.[1] What readers of Sunbeam's 1997 annual report could have found as clues to the problems involve one of the caution flags introduced in the first chapter, the relationship between accounts receivable and sales, and a new caution flag, the growth in inventories relative to sales:

(in millions)	1997	1996	% Change
Sales	$1,168.2	984.2	18.7
Receivables, net	295.6	213.4	38.5
Inventories	256.2	162.3	57.9

Source: Sunbeam 1997 Annual Report.

Between 1996 and 1997 sales grew by 19 percent, but receivables (amounts owed from credit purchases) increased by double that amount, 38.5 percent, indicating the company might not be successful in collecting on sales.[2] An even bigger caution flag for Sunbeam was the growth in inventories relative to sales: inventory increased by 58 percent in 1997, which meant the company may not have been selling the goods produced. The caution flags indicated that the company may have inflated earnings

---

[1] Harris Collingwood, "The Earnings Game: Everyone Plays, Nobody Wins," *Harvard Business Review* (June 2001).

[2] For an article discussing how to calculate a ratio based on the relationship between sales and accounts receivable to measure the degree of trouble, see Joseph T. Wells, "Irrational Ratios," *The Journal of Accountancy* (August 2001), pp. 80–83.

by recording sales that would not be collected or producing goods that would not be sold. Sunbeam ultimately had to restate earnings for 1995 through 1997 because of its revenue recognition practices and other problems, leading eventually to bankruptcy.

Revenue recognition is an area that leads to extraordinary management creativity. More discussion of the use and abuse of revenue accounting is provided later in the chapter.

GAAP: Necessary But Allowing Considerable Discretion

Although generally accepted accounting principles (GAAP) are necessary to ensure uniform standards for financial reporting, this system also allows management considerable discretion in the choices and applications of accounting policies and in the timing of revenue and expense recognition. One accounting issue that faces most companies, for example, is how to handle expenses such as buildings and equipment, which benefit the firm for many years. If the company buys a machine that is expected to last several years, all of the cost is not recorded in the year of purchase; rather, it is spread over the expected life of the machinery, "matching" the expense of the machine to the periods in which the firm will benefit from its use, with the balance of the cost recorded as an asset on the balance sheet. This process of allocating the cost of the machinery is called **depreciation.**

Several estimates and choices affect the amount of depreciation expense recognized each year, including the useful life of the machine, any salvage value expected at the end of its productivity to the firm, and a choice among several **depreciation methods.**[3] Depreciation policies affect not only the expense on the income statement but also the amount of asset recognized on the balance sheet because long-lived assets are reported net of the amount of depreciation taken (that is, the cost of asset less accumulated depreciation). To add to the confusion, two sets of rules are used for depreciation expense—one for **reporting** purposes (preparation of financial statements for public reports) and another for **tax** purposes (calculation of taxes for the government). The amounts for depreciation expense differ because the objective of tax accounting is to pay the smallest tax possible, while the objective for public reporting is to show as much income as possible or to smooth the earnings stream. Any difference between depreciation expense for reporting and tax purposes is reconciled in the financial statements through an account on the balance sheet called **deferred taxes.**

Many other judgments are made by management regarding the timing of revenues and expenses, such as when to write off an uncollectable account or write down the value of inventory that probably will not be sold. There are also circumstances in which a firm chooses policies to defer revenue recognition to a future accounting period so as not to have a huge bump in earnings during the current year or quarter. All of these decisions affect the amount of earnings reported for an accounting period.

---

[3] Straight-line depreciation allocates an equal amount of expense each year, whereas accelerated methods apportion larger amounts to the earlier years and lesser amounts to the later years. The total amount of expense is the same over the life of the asset, but the annual amount varies depending upon the estimated life, expected salvage value, and depreciation method chosen.

Time Periods

Although the life of the firm is continuous, financial statements are prepared at certain specific times, such as the end of a year or the end of a quarter. As a result, the earnings statement shows revenues, expenses, and profit or loss for that period only. The balance sheet is a "snapshot," reflecting the condition of the firm on that particular date. So the recording of a sale on December 31 rather than January 1 has an impact on both years' financial statements, as does the decision to pay off a trade account on January 1 rather than December 31.

Nonrecurring Items

Companies have transactions that are nonrecurring in nature and that do not relate to the ongoing operations of the business. Examples are the sale of a building; the write-down of impaired assets; restructuring costs, such as those associated with closing a division; or changing an accounting policy. Some of these costs, as will be discussed for Kodak, have a major impact on reported earnings.

Discretionary Costs

Many corporate expenses are discretionary in nature. Management has considerable control over the budget level and timing of expenditures for the repair and maintenance of equipment, marketing and advertising, research and development, and capital expansion. There is considerable flexibility in policies relating to the replacement of machinery, the development of new product lines, and the disposal of an unproductive operating division. Each choice regarding these discretionary costs has both a short-term and a long-term effect on profits, possibly not in the same direction.

Intangibles

For any company, there are intangible factors and qualities that affect its financial performance. These include brand awareness, product innovations, employee relations with management, the morale and efficiency of employees, the reputation of the firm with its customers, the company's prestige in its operating environment, provisions for management succession, potential exposure to changes in regulations, and publicity in the media. These qualities that affect the firm's operating success are difficult to quantify but are an essential aspect of the firm's performance, and it is important to measure them in some way.

Knowledge capital, for example, is a term used to describe the intangible human and other factors that enable a company to earn a better than average rate of return. The magazine *CFO* publishes a "Knowledge Capital Scoreboard" that ranks companies based on a quantification of these intangible values.[4]

---

[4] Andrew Osterland, "Decoding Intangibles" and "Treasures Revealed," *CFO* (April 2001), pp. 57–70.

Quality of Reported Earnings

Any discussion of accounting for financial reporting makes evident the fact that, within the framework of GAAP, management has considerable influence over the quality of earnings reported by a company. The potential exists for management to manipulate or manage earnings in a way that allows the company to meet earnings targets and show a desired pattern of earnings growth, while still following the rules.

The more conservative management is in its approach to accounting—choices, timing, and estimates—the higher is the quality of financial reporting. Sunbeam's® revenue recognition policies, for example, produced low quality earnings. The ideal is to present financial information that is useful to assess the past and predict the future. The sharper and clearer the picture presented through the financial data, and the closer that picture is to financial reality, the higher is the quality of financial statements, including reported earnings. Regardless of what a firm's management may *want* users of financial statements to believe about the company's success, the content of these chapters should help readers make a realistic assessment of a company's *actual* performance and to identify trouble spots—whether they arise because of inferior financial reporting, actual company performance, or both.[5]

STATEMENT OF EARNINGS (INCOME STATEMENT)

The "2000 Consolidated Statement of Earnings for Kodak" (Exhibit 2-1) illustrates a typical presentation of corporate earnings. For comparison purposes, companies are required to show 3-year audited statements of earnings, cash flows, and shareholders' equity; and 2-year audited statements of financial condition. The statement of earnings shows the financial results for a period of time, in this case the years ending December 31, 2000, 1999, and 1998.

Most companies, like Kodak, use the **calendar year** for financial reports. Interim statements would be prepared for each quarter, ending March 31, June 30, September 30, and December 31. Some companies adopt a **fiscal year** ending on a date other than December 31, such as January 31 or June 30.

The financial statements for Kodak are **consolidated,** which means that the information presented is a combination of the results for Kodak and its wholly owned subsidiaries. Beginning in 1998, companies were required to report **comprehensive income or loss** for the accounting period, according to the provisions of FASB Statement No. 130, "Reporting Comprehensive Income." Comprehensive income is reported either on the face of the income statement, in a separate statement of comprehensive income, or in the statement of shareholders' equity. Kodak reports comprehensive income in the statement of shareholders' equity.[6]

---

[5] For a discussion of earnings quality with a checklist of key items in the earnings statement, see Lyn M. Fraser and Aileen Ormiston, *Understanding Financial Statements,* 6th ed. (New Jersey: Prentice Hall, 2001), pp. 219–233.

[6] In addition to net income, comprehensive income includes "other comprehensive income" items relating to investments in marketable securities, pension costs, derivative financial instruments, and foreign currency adjustments.

Exhibit 2-1
Eastman Kodak Company and Subsidiary Companies
Consolidated Statement of Earnings

FOR THE YEAR ENDED DECEMBER 31, (IN MILLIONS, EXCEPT PER SHARE DATA)	2000	1999	1998
Sales	$13,994	$14,089	$13,406
Cost of goods sold	8,019	7,987	7,293
Gross profit	5,975	6,102	6,113
Selling, general and administrative expenses	2,977	3,295	3,303
Research and development costs	784	817	922
Earnings from operations	2,214	1,990	1,888
Interest expense	178	142	110
Other income (charges)	96	261	328
Earnings before income taxes	2,132	2,109	2,106
Provision for income taxes	725	717	716
Net earnings	$ 1,407	$ 1,392	$ 1,390
Basic earnings per share	$ 4.62	$ 4.38	$ 4.30
Diluted earnings per share	$ 4.59	$ 4.33	$ 4.24
Earnings used in basic and diluted earnings per share	$ 1,407	$ 1,392	$ 1,390
Number of common shares used in basic earnings per share	304.9	318.0	323.3
Incremental shares from assumed conversion of options	1.7	3.5	4.5
Number of common shares used in diluted earnings per share	306.6	321.5	327.8

The accompanying notes are an integral part of these financial statements.

Sales

Sales (or revenues) are the major source of income for most companies and the amount of sales is the first item on the earnings statement. Some companies use the designation **net sales** or **net revenues,** which means net of returns and allowances. A **sales return** is a cancellation of a sale, and a **sales allowance** is a deduction from the original sales invoice price.

A comprehensive analysis of Kodak is provided in Chapter 5, but we will also consider key individual pieces as they are discussed in each financial statement. The bumpy path of Kodak's sales revenues over the 3-year period, for instance, is an obvious problem and raises a caution flag already discussed in the first chapter, with sales and net income moving in opposite directions in 2000:

(in millions)	2000	1999	1998
Sales	$13,994	14,089	13,406
Net earnings	1,407	1,392	1,390

After a modest increase in 1999, sales declined in 2000 while net earnings increased slightly. Management's Discussion and Analysis (MD&A) section blames the 2000 sales results on deteriorating economic conditions in the second half of the year, especially impacting its consumer business, as well as the negative impact of currency, and portfolio adjustments. In contrast, sales growth in

1999 was achieved across numerous business lines. But a more fundamental question is how overall profits can improve with deteriorating sales. There will obviously be more to this story as we continue down the income statement. Kodak's stock price, perhaps reflecting these same questions and uncertainties, fell from a high of $80.38 per share in the first quarter of 1999 to a low of $35.31 in the fourth quarter of 2000.

Cost of Goods Sold

The first expense deduction from sales on the earnings statement is the cost to the seller of products or services sold to customers. This expense is called **cost of goods sold** or **cost of sales.** The amount recorded for cost of goods sold is affected by the accrual method of accounting, explained earlier in the chapter. The calculation of cost of goods sold expense is made as follows:

Beginning inventory

Plus: Purchases of goods made during the accounting period

Less: Ending inventory

Cost of goods sold expense for the accounting period

That amount shows the cost of inventory that has actually been sold. The cost of products (not services) is included in the inventory account on the balance sheet until the products are actually sold. When they are sold, the cost of the inventory is removed from the balance sheet and recorded in the cost of goods sold expense account on the earnings statement.

Cost of goods sold is also affected by the method used to value inventory, which is based on an *assumption* regarding the flow of goods and has nothing whatsoever to do with the *actual* order in which products are sold. The cost flow assumption is made to match the cost of products sold to the revenue generated from sales and to assign a dollar value to inventory remaining at the end of an accounting period. The three cost flow assumptions most frequently used are first in, first out (FIFO); last in, first out (LIFO); and average cost. The inventory cost flow assumption affects both cost of goods sold on the income statement and the inventory amount on the balance sheet, as illustrated below.

	FIFO	LIFO	Average Cost
Cost of goods sold	First goods purchased	Last goods purchased	Average of all purchases
Inventory	Last goods purchased	First goods purchased	Average of all purchases

Kodak actually uses all three methods (from Note 1, "Inventories"): "The cost of inventories in the U.S. is determined by the 'last-in, first-out' (LIFO) method. The cost of other inventories is determined by the 'first-in, first-out' (FIFO) or average cost method, which approximates current cost." Although inventories are also discussed in the next chapter, it is important to recognize here that inflation caused Kodak to report a higher earnings number due to the fact that inventories sold and accounted for under FIFO are expensed at lower costs (the first or oldest goods purchased) than the current replacement value (last or newest goods purchased).

Gross Profit

One of the key profitability measures used in analysis is the difference between sales and cost of goods sold, called **gross profit.** The **gross profit margin** is gross profit expressed as a percentage of sales:

(in millions)	2000	1999	1998
$\dfrac{\text{Gross profit}}{\text{Sales}}$	$\dfrac{\$5,975}{13,994} = 42.7\%$	$\dfrac{6,102}{14,089} = 43.3\%$	$\dfrac{6,113}{13,406} = 45.6\%$

It is evident that for Kodak the gross profit margin declined over the period, which management, in the MD&A section, attributed to falling prices, increased sales of lower margin items (like one-time use cameras and consumer digital cameras), the acquisition of a medical imaging business that had lower margins than the company's average, start-up costs in a China manufacturing project, and the negative impact of exchange rates. Kodak's cost of goods sold was also impacted by a $350 million restructuring charge taken in 1999, of which $236 million was included in cost of goods sold. Whatever the combination of causes, the result was that Kodak was generating less profit on the sale of its products.

Cost of goods sold is another area that is open to earnings management. Some companies record **fulfillment costs,** that would normally be included in cost of goods sold, as operating expenses. Amazon, for example, has expenses associated with completing a customer's order—such as warehousing, packaging, and preparing an order for shipment—that are recorded as operating rather than cost of goods sold, producing a major positive impact on the gross profit margin. In 2001, Amazon's gross profit was $798 million on sales of $3,122 million, resulting in a gross profit margin of 26 percent. Had the $374 million in fulfillment costs been included in cost of goods sold, the gross profit margin would have been cut almost in half.

Selling, General, and Administrative Expenses

This category includes expenses relating to the sale of products and services, and to the management of the business. They usually include salaries, rent, insurance, utilities, and supplies. Some firms show other costs, such as depreciation, amortization, and advertising expenses separately on the income statement, and others, like Kodak, lump them all into this one category. Finding specific dollar amounts attributed to each category requires reading notes and looking at other financial statements.

For Kodak, **depreciation** and **amortization** expense are shown on the consolidated statement of cash flows (Exhibit 1-4). As previously explained, the cost of assets (other than land, which is considered to have an unlimited useful life) that will benefit a firm for more than 1 year is allocated over the asset's service life. **Depreciation** is used to allocate the cost of tangible assets such as buildings, machinery, equipment, furnishings, and vehicles. **Amortization** is the process used for intangible assets such as patents, copyrights, trademarks, licenses, and franchises; it was formerly used to allocate the cost of goodwill, but that rule has recently been changed and will be explained more fully in connection with the discussion of goodwill on Kodak's statement of financial condition. The cost of acquiring and developing natural resources—oil, gas, other minerals, standing timber—is allocated through **depletion.**

Advertising expense for Kodak is quantified under Note 1 to the financial statements. "Advertising costs are expensed as incurred and included in selling, general and administrative (SG&A) expenses. Advertising expenses amounted to $701 million, $717 million and $765 million in 2000, 1999, and 1998, respectively." Kodak *decreased* its expenditures for advertising—a discretionary expense. The explanation provided in its "Management Discussion and Analysis" section for the overall reduction in SG&A expenses is that the reduced expenditures reflect "success in cost reduction initiatives" and in "portfolio actions," such as a divestiture, but there is no specific explanation for the reductions in advertising expense. If the 1998 budget level for advertising had been maintained, Kodak's pretax profit in 2000 would have been $64 million lower. The concern for analysis is whether reductions in advertising and other discretionary costs may ultimately result in lower sales and earnings.

Research and Development Costs

Research and development (R&D) is another discretionary expense for Kodak which, like advertising, is critical to ongoing success in this industry. This item is shown separately on the Kodak earnings statement and, like advertising, declined over the 3-year period from $922 million in 1998 to $817 million in 1999 to $784 million in 2000. Management attributed the reduction in costs to the divestiture of Eastman Software, improvement in the R&D cost structure, a more tightly focused portfolio, and more joint development with more work shared by partners. Had the R&D budget remained at 1998 levels, operating profit would have been negatively impacted by $105 million before taxes in 1999 and $138 million in 2000.

Earnings from Operations

Operating profit is the second stage of profit measurement on the earnings statement. This figure provides the basis for assessing the success of a company in its normal, ongoing business operations, apart from financing and investing activities and separate from tax considerations. The **operating profit margin** shows the relationship between operating profit and sales:

(in millions)	2000	1999	1998
$\dfrac{\text{Operating profit}}{\text{Sales}}$	$\dfrac{\$2,214}{13,994} = 15.8\%$	$\dfrac{1,990}{14,089} = 14.1\%$	$\dfrac{1,888}{13,406} = 14.1\%$

Here, Kodak showed improvement. The cost reductions, management efficiencies, and divestitures had a positive impact on operating profit—at least in the short run.

Interest Expense

Interest expense is the amount paid each year on borrowed funds and showed a steady increase for Kodak partly because interest rates rose but mostly because borrowings have increased to finance capital additions. The amount of debt is shown in the liabilities section of the "Consolidated Statement of Financial Position" (Exhibit 1-2), with specific detail on debt provided in notes.

Other Income (Charges)

This category typically includes revenues and costs other than from operations, such as dividend and interest income, gains (losses) from the sale of investments, income (loss) from investments, write-downs from asset impairments, and gains (losses) from the sale of assets. These amounts can significantly affect a company's overall income for the period, as they did for Kodak, which shows a decreasing trend over the 3-year period:

(in millions)	2000	1999	1998
Other income (charges)	$ 96	261	328

Some explanation was offered in the MD&A section, which listed gains from the sale of a division, equity earnings (see Box 2-1), special charges, and gains on asset sales as part of other income. But it is not possible from reading the notes to the financial statements or MD&A to determine exactly how this figure was calculated, and that is a problem, given the magnitude of the figure.

Earnings Before Income Taxes—Provision for Income Tax

The next step of profit measurement on the Kodak statement of earnings is the amount of earnings before income taxes. As previously explained, the amount of income tax expense reported in the earnings statement is not the same as the amount of taxes actually paid because accounting rules differ from tax laws. The income tax expense figure shown in the earnings statement is the amount based on rules for accounting purposes. The difference between the two amounts is shown as deferred tax on the statement of financial condition. Kodak has maintained a constant average tax rate of 34 percent.

(in millions)	2000	1999	1998
$\dfrac{\text{Provision for income taxes}}{\text{Earnings before income tax}}$	$\dfrac{\$725}{2{,}132} = 34.0\%$	$\dfrac{717}{2{,}109} = 34.0\%$	$\dfrac{716}{2{,}106} = 34.0\%$

Net Earnings

Net income or the "bottom line" represents the firm's profit after consideration of all revenue and expense reported for an accounting period. When a company announces its "earnings" for the year or the quarter, this is the figure being reported. **The net profit margin** is a commonly used financial ratio that shows the percentage

BOX 2-1
Accounting for Investments

Accounting for corporate investments is a complex subject, and although a full explanation is beyond the scope of this book, some background is helpful in understanding what is reported in the financial statements. One company buys shares in another firm's voting stock with the intention of earning a return on its investment. There are several types and levels of investment that are reflected in corporate financial statements. If the investor company holds more than 50 percent ownership of the investee firm's voting stock, the investor company (parent) clearly controls the investee company (subsidiary). The parent company prepares **consolidated financial statements** as if the two entities are one. As indicated in Note 1 to the Kodak financial statements, "The consolidated financial statements include the accounts of Eastman Kodak Company and its majority owned subsidiary companies."

When one firm owns less than 20 percent of another, the investments are usually assumed to be for speculative purposes and are carried on the statement of financial condition (balance sheet) as **marketable securities.** Income recognition depends upon the intention of the investor; these investments are discussed in Chapter 3.

If the company's investment falls between 20 percent and 50 percent, the situation becomes less clearcut because the degree of control is not obvious. Accounting rules defining the circumstances under which one company controls another are undergoing revision, but the issue is how to account for investments of less than 50 percent. The **equity method** allows the investor proportionate recognition of the investee's net income (loss), whether or not any dividends are paid, and is used when the investor company can exercise *significant influence* over the investee company's operating and investing policies. Under the **cost method,** the investor recognizes only income to the extent of cash dividends received. Although there are exceptions, 20 percent ownership of voting stock is generally considered to be evidence of substantial influence. Although the accounting detail is not discussed here, it is important to note that the method used affects both income (loss) recognized in the earnings statement of the investor company and the amount shown for the investment on the balance sheet. Note 1 to the Kodak financial statements includes the following: "The equity method of accounting is used for investments in associated companies over which Kodak does not have effective control."

of profit earned on every dollar of sales, with Kodak's at around 10 percent, or 10 cents profit for every $1 of sales:[7]

(in millions)	2000	1999	1998
$\dfrac{\text{Net earnings}}{\text{Sales}}$	$\dfrac{\$1,407}{13,994} = 10.1\%$	$\dfrac{1,392}{14,089} = 9.9\%$	$\dfrac{1,390}{13,406} = 10.4\%$

The following section on which earnings figure to use has much more discussion on Kodak's profit performance.

---

[7] Numbers may not match those in the common-size statement shown in Exhibit 2-2 due to rounding.

Basic and Diluted Earnings per Share

Earnings per share reports the firm's net income for every common stock share. Companies with complex capital structures—which means that there are convertible securities (bonds or preferred stock convertible into common stock), stock options, or warrants—report two amounts for earnings per share: **basic** and **diluted.** Basic uses the weighted-average number of common shares currently outstanding. Diluted assumes the amount of common shares that would be outstanding if convertible securities were converted into common stock and/or the options and warrants were exercised. The dual presentation is shown for Kodak, and the number of shares used in the calculations is also presented. In Kodak's case, the dilution reflects assumed exercise and conversion of employee stock options.

Evaluating the quality of earnings reported by a company should include a consideration of any material change in the number of shares outstanding. A company wants to report steadily increasing earnings per share, which Kodak is able to do:

	2000	1999	1998
Basic earnings per share	$4.62	4.38	4.30

But also note that Kodak has been steadily reducing the number of shares outstanding:

(in millions)	2000	1999	1997
Number of common shares	304.9	318.0	323.3

Changes in the number of shares outstanding result from transactions such as treasury stock (company purchases its own shares for purposes such as employee stock option plans) or from the purchase and retirement of shares. The increasing earnings per share figure for Kodak is somewhat misleading because of these reductions in the number of shares used in the calculation.

Extraordinary Items, Discontinued Operations, and Accounting Changes

Certain special items must be reported separately on the earnings statement if they occur during an accounting period. These include **discontinued operations, extraordinary transactions,** and the **cumulative effect of changes in accounting principles.** Discontinued operations occur when a firm sells a major portion of a business, which did happen for Kodak in 1996 (Exhibit 2-2), associated with the sale of nonimaging health businesses. The results of continuing operations are shown separately from the operating results of the discontinued portion of the business. Any gain or loss on the disposal is also shown separately. Extraordinary gains and losses are items that are unusual in nature and not expected to recur in the foreseeable future, considering the firm's operating environment. The cumulative effect of a change in accounting principle is disclosed when a firm changes an accounting policy; for example, one that is mandated by the accounting rule-makers.

Exhibit 2-2 shows a 5-year **common size income statement** for Kodak, a form of the statement that facilitates the analysis of a firm's performance for each year in var-

Exhibit 2-2

Eastman Kodak Company Common Size Income Statements (Percent)

	2000	1999	1998	1997	1996
Sales	100.0	100.0	100.0	100.0	100.0
Cost of goods sold	57.3	56.7	54.4	54.9	52.1
Gross profit	42.7	43.3	45.6	45.1	47.9
Selling, general & administrative	21.3	23.4	24.6	26.9	27.6
Research & development costs	5.6	5.8	6.9	8.5	6.4
Restructuring costs & asset impair.	0.0	0.0	0.0	8.9	2.3
Earnings from operations	15.8	14.1	14.1	0.8	11.6
Interest expense	(1.3)	(1.0)	(0.8)	(0.7)	(0.5)
Other income (charges)	0.7	1.9	2.4	0.2	(1.3)
Earnings before income taxes	15.2	15.0	15.7	0.3	9.8
Provision for income taxes	5.2	5.1	5.3	0.3	3.4
Earnings from continuing operations	10.0	9.9	10.4	0.0	6.4
Gain on sale of discontinued ops.	0.0	0.0	0.0	0.0	1.7
Net earnings	10.0	9.9	10.4	0.0	8.1

ious categories and trends over time by expressing each item on the income statement as a percentage of sales. This 5-year summary illustrates the decreasing trend in gross profit but shows the improvements in operating earnings resulting from relative reductions in operating expenses. Over the 5-year period, Kodak has had proportionate increases in interest expense, decreases in other income, but overall improvement in net earnings because of the operating cost savings.

Which Earnings Figure to Use

With all the available possibilities, the question is which earnings figure to use in evaluating a firm's past performance—always with the objective of projecting where the company is headed in the future. The place to start is at the bottom, with net income, which is the conventional measure of success:

Net Income

	2000	1999	1998
Net earnings (in millions)	$1,407	1,392	1,390
Percent increase	1.1%	0.1%	

Kodak, as shown at the beginning of the chapter, has had a small but steady increase in earnings, and that's what looks good to investors. Although the increase in percentage terms is very slight, less than 1 percent in 1999 and 1.1 percent in 2000, the movement is still in the right direction. Kodak has achieved its objective of demonstrating stable earnings growth. But is it believable?

Earnings Before Interest, Taxes, Depreciation, and Amortization (EBITDA)

Another way of looking at profit is something some firms call "cash earnings," which takes conventional operating profit and adds back the noncash charges—depreciation and amortization—producing a widely used profit measure called EBITDA. The depreciation and amortization charges are "noncash" because, as explained earlier, they are allocations of a cost previously made. EBITDA for Kodak is calculated as follows:

(in millions)	2000	1999	1998
Earnings from operations	$2,214	1,990	1,888
+ Depreciation and amortization	889	918	853
EBITDA	$3,103	2,908	2,741
Percent increase	6.7%	6.1%	

EBITDA looks even better than net income, with increases of over 6 percent in both years. Some companies announce EBITDA in their earnings report rather than earnings calculated by generally accepted accounting principles or hype EBITDA while minimizing the importance of GAAP net income.

Blockbuster, which reported losses in each of the 3 years from 1998 through 2000, includes EBITDA as an item in a table of its "Consolidated Results." In contrast to losses of $337 (1998), $69 (1999), and $76 (2000) million in each of the 3 years, EBITDA is a positive $24, $514, and $535 million. In a note, EBITDA is explained as "additional information about our operations" and "may differ in the method of calculation from similarly titled measures used by other companies."

It is important to understand that EBITDA, even though sometimes called "cash earnings," is not the same as cash generated from operations. Also, the amount of depreciation added back in calculating EBITDA, as explained above, is affected by factors such as the estimated useful life of the equipment and choice of depreciation method. Companies with long-lived assets will have relatively lower depreciation charges, for example, than those with short-lived assets, which makes comparison of EBITDA figures among industries difficult. EBITDA also can be misleading to a prospective lender because it ignores existing debt by not including interest expense. Another problem is that EBITDA ignores the quality of reported earnings; like net earnings, this figure can be readily "managed" by management.[8]

Operating Profit

The figure for earnings from operations, without the add-backs for noncash charges, is another possible performance measure because this figure should reflect the firm's performance from its basic business operations:

(in millions)	2000	1999	1998
Earnings from operations	$2,214	1,990	1,888
Percent increase	11.3%	5.4%	

---

[8] For an enlightening analysis of EBITDA, see Herb Greenberg, "Alphabet Dupe: Why Ebitda Falls Short," *Fortune* (July 10, 2000), pp. 240–41.

Kodak steadily improved its operating performance by 5 percent in 1999 and 11 percent in 2000. This way of measuring performance appears even better than the previous two possibilities. But wait. Why did operating profit grow so much faster than net income, and what might that mean? A look through the figures on the income statement shows that the reasons are increases in "interest expense" and decreases in "other income." Interest expense has grown, in part because of rising interest rates but mostly because Kodak needed to borrow more. Kodak's statement of financial position shows that both short-term and long-term borrowings have increased. Further, Kodak's figure for "other income," as previously explained, includes all sorts of confusions like investment income and the impact of selling assets and entire divisions.

Operating Profit, aka Pro Forma Earnings and Core Earnings

There are numerous variations on the theme of operating profit as recorded on the earnings statements, all attempting to measure the firm's success in generating earnings from its ongoing sales of goods and/or services. The terms **pro forma earnings** or **core earnings** are two of the alternative figures for operating profits. Each adjusts net income in some way for items not expected to be part of ongoing business operations.

"Pro forma" has also been a term used to describe the projections of financial statements, often used by creditors in making lending decisions. Bankers look at projections of financial statements, called pro forma statements, as if the loan were made based on certain assumptions about the future. In the 1990s pro forma became a widely used measure of operating performance, particularly for start-up companies such as dot-coms. Pro forma earnings exclude certain items that are used in calculating net income, but there is no uniform definition of pro forma earnings, even within a single company that may report more than one set of pro forma earnings.

For the quarter ending September 30, 2001, Nortel Networks provided three different earnings figures. By conventional accounting rules, Nortel lost $1.08 per share for the quarter. Using one pro forma measurement that excluded "special charges," such as acquisition and restructuring costs, Nortel's quarterly loss was only 68 cents per share. Best of all was the pro forma calculation that produced a loss of only 27 cents per share by also eliminating some "incremental charges," such as write-downs of inventory.[9] Amazon's press release announcing third quarter earnings for 2001 leads with a report that the pro forma loss from operations improved 60 percent to $27 million. The only reference to its GAAP loss of $170 million comes as the ninth item in a bulleted list later in the press release.

Kodak's Big Bath

Kodak has its own version of alternate earnings, provided in the "Management's Discussion and Analysis" section. The company's results for the 3 years, 1998 through 2000, included a number of significant adjustments, as shown in Exhibit 2-3.

---

[9] Nanette Byrnes and David Henry, "Confused About Earnings?" *Business Week* (November 26, 2001), pp. 77–84.

Exhibit 2-3

Adjustments to Kodak's Earnings

2000

—A pretax charge of $50 million ($33 million after tax) associated with the sale and exit of a manufacturing facility.

Excluding the above, *net earnings were $1,440 million.*

1999

—A pretax restructuring charge of $350 million ($232 million after tax) related to worldwide manufacturing and photofinishing consolidation and reductions in selling, general and administrative positions worldwide.

—Pretax charges of $11 million ($7 million after tax) related to accelerated depreciation of assets still in use during 1999 and sold in 2000 in connection with the exit of one of the Company's manufacturing facilities.

—Pretax charges totaling approximately $103 million ($68 million after tax) associated with business exits and the write-off of the company's Calcomp investment which was determined to be unrecoverable.

—Pretax gains of $120 million ($79 million after tax) related to the sale of divisions.

Excluding the above items, *net earnings were $1,619 million.*

1998

—Pretax gains of $87 million ($57 million after tax) and $66 million ($44 million after tax) for sales of a subsidiary and an investment.

—A pretax charge of $132 million ($87 million after tax) for asset write-downs and employee severance.

—A pretax charge of $45 million ($30 after tax) primarily for in-process research and development associated with the acquisition of a business.

Excluding the above items and pretax litigation charges of $35 million ($23 million after tax), *net earnings were $1,429 million.*

The following table shows Kodak's earnings adjusted for the previous charges and gains compared with earnings as reported in the statement of earnings:

(in millions)	Net Earnings, Adjusted	Net Earnings, Reported	Difference
2000	$ 1,440	1,407	–33
1999	1,619	1,392	–227
1998	1,429	1,390	–39

Kodak's reported earnings were lower in each of the 3 years as a result of these transactions, but especially so in 1999. Companies have considerable discretion in the timing of the kinds of gains and losses that contribute to these figures. When a company takes enormous write-offs in one period, called a **big bath,** the firm may be doing so in order to improve profits in future years. This is certainly the effect on Kodak's earnings. Without the "big bath," Kodak's earnings would have *decreased* between 1999 and 2000 from $1,619 million to $1,440 million, rather than showing the *increase* that Kodak was able to report from $1,392 million to $1,407 in 2000.

Kodak is not the only company using the big bath strategy. For the quarter ending April 28, 2001, Cisco® Systems recognized restructuring costs and other special charges of $1.2 billion and inventory write-downs of $2.2 billion, contributing to a loss for the quarter of $2.7 billion. Cisco reported a pro forma profit for the quarter of $230 million by excluding special charges. Further, as a result of taking the big bath all in one quarter, Cisco was also able to announce a small GAAP profit of $7 million for the following quarter, ending July 28, 2001.

These alternative earnings calculations are attempts to develop a figure for operating earnings that eliminates noncash charges and/or eliminates one-time transactions, which might be considered events of the past and thus not indicative of future potential. But there is no uniform way of figuring this new amount for operating profit. Standard & Poor's has proposed a specific set of rules for calculating operating earnings that includes the costs of purchases, research and development, restructuring expenses, write-downs from continuing operations, and the cost to the company of stock options; the S&P figure would not include expenses related to mergers and acquisitions, impairment of goodwill, litigation settlements, and gains or losses on asset sales.[10]

Cash Flow from Operations

The figure for cash earnings that *is* calculated in a uniform way, using generally accepted accounting principles, is "cash flow from operations" or "cash flow from operating activities," shown on the "Consolidated Statement of Cash Flows" (Exhibit 1-4). This measure of performance adjusts accrual-based net income into a cash figure. As discussed in the first chapter for Enron, positive net income is meaningless unless the company can turn its earnings into cash because it is cash that a company needs to grow and to meet its obligations. Analysts are increasingly relying on cash flow from operations rather than net income as a bottom-line measure of performance.[11] In other words, that means we have saved the best for last.

Adding cash flow from operating activities to the list, there are now at least five possible earnings figures to consider in evaluating Kodak's 1998–2000 performance:

(in millions)	2000	1999	1998
Net earnings	$1,407	1,392	1,390
EBITDA	3,103	2,908	2,741
Earnings from operations	2,214	1,990	1,888
Earnings adjusted for special gains and charges	1,440	1,619	1,429
Cash flow provided by operating activities	982	1,933	1,483

The cash flow figure reveals that Kodak generated cash in all 3 years; but for 2000, the amount of cash generated from operations is far less than in the 2 previous years

---

[10] Byrnes and Henry, *Ibid.*, p. 80.
[11] For example, see Elizabeth MacDonald, "Analysts Increasingly Favor Using Cash Flow Over Reported Earnings in Stock Valuations," *The Wall Street Journal* (April 1, 1999), p. C2.

and is lower than the amount of earnings reported for 2000. That helps explain why Kodak had to increase both short-term and long-term borrowing, thus driving up interest expense. There is more discussion of cash flow from operations and its usefulness as an analytical tool in Chapters 4 and 5.

What readers of annual reports and of earnings press releases need to be aware of when looking at various measures of profit is how they are calculated and what the figures mean. Although there is no definitive answer to the question of what earnings figure to use, it is obvious that the emphasis in this book is on cash flow from operations. At the same time, it is important to understand that evaluating a company's performance should never rely on any one single measure of performance.

COOKING THE BOOKS

This final section of the chapter on earnings describes some of the additional "earnings-enhancement" techniques that readers may encounter when studying annual reports. According to a study released in mid-2001 by the Financial Executives International Research Foundation on the quality of financial reporting, there were 1,080 restatements of earnings during the period between 1977 and 2000, but more than half of those occurred during the last 3 years of the study—1998, 1999, and 2000. The most common reason for the restatements, accounting for one-third of the cases, was revenue recognition. Cost issues, usually relating to inventory valuation, were the second most common cause.[12]

The SEC issued "Staff Accounting Bulletin 101" in 1999 with the intention of providing guidance on the recognition, presentation, and disclosure of revenue, but the impact of this ruling has been minimal.[13] In January 2002, the Financial Accounting Standards Board (FASB) discussed the objective and scope of a potential major project on the recognition of revenue and liabilities in financial statements. The FASB has issued a project proposal for public comment, and this project could ultimately lead to a new accounting standard on revenue recognition. The process is lengthy, however, and it sometimes takes several years for the FASB to make decisions on new accounting rules. It is also possible that the congressional hearings currently taking place on accounting and reporting issues following Enron's collapse will produce new accounting and auditing standards.

The creative techniques used by company managements come in a wide assortment of approaches, some with their own names, such as the **big bath** described for Kodak, **channel stuffing,** and **barter.**[14] Channel stuffing is a practice

---

[12] *Study of Financial Reporting Quality,* Financial Executives International Research Foundation (June 2001).

[13] Jonathan Weil, "Many Companies Fail to Heed the SEC On Its Revenue-Recognition Guidelines," *The Wall Street Journal* (December 14, 2000), pp. C1 and C4.

[14] Among the many interesting articles on this topic are Harris Collingwood, "The Earnings Game: Everyone Plays, Nobody Wins," *Harvard Business Review* (June 2001); Andy Kessler, "Creative Accounting.com," *The Wall Street Journal* (July 24, 2000); David Henry, "The Numbers Game," *Business Week* (May 14, 2001); and "Presto Chango! Sales are Huge!" *Fortune* (March 20, 2000).

used to encourage customers to purchase more products than they need or goods they are not ready to buy. Sunbeam's winter sale of outdoor barbecue grills, discussed earlier in the chapter, is a classic example. A variation on this theme is **vendor financing,** when a company lends money to its customers so that they can buy products. Motorola's 10-K report for 2000 includes the following: "The competitive environment in which Motorola operates requires Motorola and many of its principal competitors to provide significant amounts of medium-term and long-term customer financing. Customer financing arrangements may include all or a portion of the purchase price for Motorola's products and services, as well as working capital." Motorola disclosed in its first quarter 2001 10-Q filing with the SEC that approximately $2 billion of its $2.7 billion finance receivables related to one customer, Telsim, in Turkey. When $728 million of the note came due in April, Telsim did not pay. Motorola's stock has reflected the impact of this transaction, falling from a high of $57.58 in March 2000 when the loan was announced to as low as $11.50 in April 2001.

Barter allows companies to record revenues on deals not involving cash—for example, the exchange of advertising space on a Web page for advertisements on radio and television, or the exchange of Web site ads of one company on another's Web site. Online companies, especially start-ups, commonly derive a portion of their revenues from barter transactions. These arrangements are disclosed in management's discussion and analysis, such as the following in the 2000 annual report for SportsLine—barter transactions, in which the company received advertising or other services or goods in exchange for content or advertising on its Web sites, accounted for approximately 17 percent of total revenue for 2000. StarMedia® Technology, a masterful user of bartering, was delisted from the NASDAQ in February 2002.

Another tactic is to boost revenues by including in sales the **gross price** of items sold even though the company will retain only a portion of the sales amount. Priceline.com®, which markets airline tickets, hotel rooms, and rental cars on the Web, grosses up its sales revenue by counting as revenue the full price of an airline ticket even though most of that is owed to the airline. In 2000, Priceline.com had travel revenues of $1,217 million, but $1,040 million was paid back to airlines, hotels, and car rental agencies, so its actual revenue was only $177 million, over $1 billion less than reported.

There are many other demonstrated strategies for managing earnings. Companies improve reported income by changing assumptions about the useful life of assets and the collectibility of receivables. If the estimated useful life of an asset is extended, for example, depreciation expense decreases. Or if a firm assumes fewer customers will default on payments, the doubtful account expense is reduced. Unlike the amount paid for salaries, the cost of employee stock options does not have to be deducted from income; the effect on shareholders' equity is discussed in Chapter 3, as is the impact of accounting for pensions, which can have a major impact on earnings.

When earnings were growing too fast at W. R. Grace in the 1990s, the profits were stashed away in a **reserve account** to be used in later years to mask declining earnings. The accounting games came to light in 1999 when the SEC and a whistle blower filed suits against the firm for fraudulent accounting practices. W. R. Grace's independent auditors Price Waterhouse told the company the practice was wrong but gave the financial statements a clean report.[15] Xerox® had to restate 1997–2000 earnings because of several inappropriate accounting practices, including the improper use of a reserve account to offset unrelated expenses. **Premature revenue recognition** is another earnings-enhancement tactic. MicroStrategy®, for example, sold long-term software services to customers and booked all the revenue for the period in which the sale was made, and had to restate earnings for 1998 and 1999, causing its stock to plummet dramatically.

Signals Blinking

Uncovering the specific practices previously described requires careful reading of notes to the financial statements and management's discussion and analysis, but it is helpful to know that companies that do squirrelly things with accounting usually have one or more caution flags emitting signals. Sunbeam®, as already illustrated, had its receivables and inventory growing much faster than sales. Enron's growth rates in revenues and earnings were dramatically different in 2000, the year before its bankruptcy, with revenues increasing by 251 percent but net income by less than 10 percent. Motorola's sales grew by 14 percent in 2000 and 6 percent in 1999, whereas net income increased 48 percent and 198 percent in those 2 years. Microstrategy, Blockbuster, Amazon, and Sportsline all reported a large growth in sales between 1999 and 2000, but *increases* in bottom-line *losses*. At Xerox®, before required restatements, sales *decreased* in 1999 whereas net income *rose* by 360 percent.

Finally, it should be noted that not all companies attempt to mislead the users of financial report information. The authors hope that this book helps readers to identify clarity and fairness in financial statement presentations as well as to recognize the devices for cooking the books.

READERS' CHECKLIST OF CAUTION FLAGS
FROM CHAPTER 2

➤ Revenue and earnings growing at substantially different rates or moving in opposite directions

➤ Accounts receivable and/or inventories growing much faster than sales

➤ Large, unexplained reductions in discretionary items such as advertising, research and development

➤ Profit margins shrinking or growing dramatically or moving in opposite directions

➤ Earnings reports featuring "pro forma" and other earnings figures that are not prepared according to generally accepted accounting principles

➤ Showing more than one pro forma earnings amount

➤ Taking large, one-time (special) charges against earnings

➤ Increasing reserves without justification

➤ Reducing the allowance for doubtful accounts when sales and accounts receivable are rising

➤ Changing accounting estimates and assumptions

---

[15] Ann Davis, "Grace Case Illustrates Earnings 'Management'," *The Wall Street Journal* (April 7, 1999), pp. C1, C22.

Solutions are provided immediately following the Glossary at the end of the book.

1. Which of the following statements is true about the accrual basis of accounting?
    a. Expenses are recorded when cash is paid.
    b. Revenues are recorded when earned and expenses are recorded when incurred regardless of when cash is received or paid out.
    c. Accrual basis accounting is based on the matching principle that measures earnings by matching assets to liabilities.
    d. Both (b) and (c)

2. What is the process of allocating the cost of assets such as buildings and equipment called?
    a. GAAP
    b. Deferred taxes
    c. Discretionary allocation
    d. Depreciation

3. Which of the following would be considered a nonrecurring item?
    a. Sale of a building
    b. Research and development
    c. Salaries
    d. Advertising

4. What are costs over which management has considerable control with regard to the level and timing of the expenditures?
    a. Intangibles
    b. Knowledge capital
    c. Earnings management
    d. Discretionary costs

5. Generally, what are the first two accounts appearing on an income statement?
    a. Sales and cost of goods sold
    b. Sales and purchases of goods
    c. Sales returns and sales allowances
    d. Net revenues and net expenses

6. What is the calculation of cost of goods sold expense?
    a. Inventory + purchases = cost of goods sold
    b. Beginning inventory – purchases – ending inventory = cost of goods sold
    c. Beginning inventory + purchases – ending inventory = cost of goods sold
    d. None of the above

7. What does gross profit measure?
    a. Sales less fulfillment costs
    b. Sales less cost of goods sold
    c. Sales less all operating costs
    d. Sales less returns

8. How are operating costs other than cost of goods sold shown in income statements?
    a. They are shown in the notes to the financial statements.
    b. Operating costs are not shown on the income statement.

c. Firms may show certain expenses separately and all others in a category labeled selling, general, and administrative expenses.

d. Operating costs are lumped together with cost of goods sold.

9. Why is the operating profit figure important?

a. This figure provides the basis for assessing the success of a company in its normal, ongoing business operations, apart from financing and investing activities and separate from tax considerations.

b. This figure provides the basis for assessing the success of a company after consideration of all items of revenue and expense.

c. This figure allows the user to not only assess the success of the ongoing operations of the company, but also the amount of cash generated.

d. This figure allows the user to assess the success of the company without the clutter of such items as discretionary costs and nonrecurring items.

10. Which of the following items would most likely be included in the category "other income (charges)"?

a. Advertising expense, gains on asset sales, and depreciation

b. Depreciation, amortization, and equity earnings

c. Interest expense, sale of investments, cost of goods sold

d. Dividend income, interest income, equity earnings

11. How do the equity and cost methods used for accounting for investments differ?

a. The equity method is used for investments in which the investor firm has 50 percent or more ownership in the investee, and the cost method is used when there is less than 50 percent ownership.

b. Under the equity method, investments are recorded in the marketable securities account, and under the cost method, investments are recorded in the long-term investments account.

c. The equity method allows the investor proportionate recognition of the investee's net income, whereas the cost method allows recognition of the investee's income only to the extent that cash dividends are received by the investing firm.

d. Both (a) and (c)

12. Why is the income tax expense reported on the income statement different than the amount of tax actually paid?

a. Accounting rules differ from tax laws.

b. Companies generally lie on their tax returns, but report the correct number in the income statement.

c. Companies have to have a fiscal year ending December 31 for tax purposes, but may choose a different fiscal year for reporting purposes.

d. Companies must maintain a 34 percent average tax rate.

13. How does net profit differ from operating profit?

a. The difference is the amount of tax expense.

b. Operating profit includes interest expense and net profit does not.

c. Operating profit is calculated before interest expense, other income or charges, and taxes, whereas net profit includes all of those items.

d. Net profit represents the firm's profit after consideration of all revenue and expense reported for an accounting period, whereas operating profit only considers sales revenue and cost of goods sold.

14. How is it possible for a company to create an upward trend in the earnings per share figure?
    a. The company can include a diluted earnings per share number that assumes that all convertible securities have been converted to shares of common stock.
    b. The company can repurchase its own shares of common stock so fewer shares of stock are outstanding.
    c. The company can use a weighted average number of common shares outstanding when calculating the earnings per share numbers.
    d. There is no way for a company to purposely create an upward trend in this figure.
15. What items must be presented separately on the earnings statement?
    a. Advertising expense, research and development, repairs and maintenance
    b. Discontinued operations, GAAP, advertising expense
    c. Extraordinary transactions, EBITDA, cash flow provided by operating activities
    d. Discontinued operations, extraordinary transactions, and cumulative effect of changes in accounting principles
16. What is a common size income statement?
    a. A statement that expresses each item on the income statement as a percentage of sales
    b. A statement that expresses each item on the income statement as a percentage of assets
    c. A statement that expresses each item on the income statement as a percentage of net earnings
    d. A statement to facilitate the use of common sense when analyzing the income statement
17. Why can EBITDA be a misleading figure?
    a. This figure ignores debt by not including interest expense.
    b. This figure can be readily managed by management.
    c. Not all companies calculate EBITDA the same way.
    d. All of the above
18. Why do companies like to employ the "big bath" strategy?
    a. This strategy allows companies to clean up their books.
    b. By taking enormous write-offs in one year, the following year's profit may appear to be much better.
    c. A big bath will ensure profitability in subsequent years.
    d. Companies don't like big baths any more than most children.
19. Which earnings figure is the best number for investors to use in making decisions?
    a. Earnings adjusted for special gains and charges.
    b. Cash flow provided by operating activities.
    c. Investors should not use any of the earnings numbers, because they are usually misleading.
    d. There is no definitive answer, except that investors should not rely on any one single measure of performance.

Chapter 3

Assets, Liabilities, and Equity: What a Firm Owns and Owes

➤ *Statement of financial condition/balance sheet*

➤ *Statement of shareholders' equity*

➤ *Loose screws scattered throughout chapter: Inadequate UV protection, hidden debt, pension plethora, compensating with options— who pays?*

➤ *Caution flags for users of annual reports*

➤ *Test yourself*

Although this chapter covers two new financial statements—the statement of financial condition (or balance sheet) and the statement of shareholders' equity—the discussion builds on material presented in the previous chapter because the four financial statements are interconnected. When a sale is made and the revenue recognized, all of the financial statements are affected, not just the earnings statement. On the balance sheet, cash or accounts receivable increase, depending upon whether it is a cash or credit sale. The inventory account is reduced on the balance sheet as cost of goods sold expense is recorded in the earnings statement. The profit (or loss) on the sale shows up as a change in equity, and the cash portion of the transaction is recorded as cash flow from operations on the cash flow statement.

This chapter takes readers through Kodak's Statement of Financial Position and very briefly covers the Statement of Shareholders' Equity. In the process, we continue to explore not only the content of the statements but how to interpret the material presented.

The accounts on the balance sheet are integral to any comprehensive analysis of a company's condition and performance. Consider, for instance, the **inventory** account. Sales of inventory are the largest source of revenue for many firms. Inventory is an essential component of **liquidity** analysis, which considers the ability of the firm to meet cash needs as they arise. Changes in inventory balances from one period to the next can significantly affect cash flow from operations. Write-downs in the value of inventory have already been discussed as one of the special charges that may have a significant impact on profit, and improper inventory valuation has also been a major cause of earnings restatements.

Prior to its bankruptcy in 2000, Styling Technology, an Arizona-based beauty products manufacturer, hired Arthur Andersen to audit a company called Body Drench, which Styling Technology planned to purchase. Andersen's work included inspections of Body Drench's football-field size product warehouse in Tennessee, and the Andersen accountants verified the product amounts. When Styling Technology executives inspected the inventory after purchasing the company, 80 percent of Body Drench's tanning lotions turned out to be outdated. Some barrels labeled "lotion" were actually filled with water, and some aisles were stocked with obsolete Christmas merchandise. Rows and rows of products were not suitable for sale.[1]

Although we cannot guarantee you a suntan, this chapter covers such issues as the valuation of inventory and its relationship to earnings. The same approach is used to explain and interpret the other key accounts on a statement of financial condition.

STATEMENT OF FINANCIAL CONDITION (BALANCE SHEET)

Exhibit 3-1 shows the Consolidated Statement of Financial Position for Eastman Kodak Company and Subsidiary Companies on December 31, 2000, and 1999. Although the accounts shown on Kodak's statement of financial condition vary somewhat from other firms and industries, those described in the chapter are common to most companies.

The statement of financial condition is a summary of what the firm owns **(assets)** and owes—to outsiders **(liabilities)** and owners **(shareholders' equity).** It is prepared at a point in time—a specific date—such as the end of the year or the quarter, in contrast to the other three financial statements that are prepared for a period of time. By definition, the account balances on a balance sheet must balance; the total of all assets equals the sum of liabilities and shareholders' equity:

Assets = Liabilities + Shareholders' Equity.

When a transaction increases an asset, there must be a corresponding increase in a liability or equity account, or a decrease in another asset account, or some combination of changes that keeps each side the same. If the company borrows from the bank to purchase equipment, the equipment account (asset) increases and the notes payable account (liability) also increases by the same amount. As payments are made, the cash account (asset) and notes payable account (liability) are reduced in equal amounts. At all times, the balance sheet stays in balance.

---

[1]   David Dietz, "Insider Accuses Andersen of Fraud," *The Arizona Republic* (January 14, 2002), pp. D1, D4.

Exhibit 3-1

Eastman Kodak Company and Subsidiary Companies
Consolidated Statement of Financial Position

At December 31, (in millions, except share and per share data)	2000	1999
Assets		
Current Assets		
Cash and cash equivalents	$ 246	$ 373
Marketable securities	5	20
Receivables	2,653	2,537
Inventories	1,718	1,519
Deferred income tax charges	575	689
Other	294	306
Total current assets	5,491	5,444
Properties		
Land, buildings and equipment at cost	12,963	13,289
Less: Accumulated depreciation	7,044	7,342
Net properties	5,919	5,947
Other Assets		
Goodwill (net of accumulated amortization of $778 and $671)	947	982
Long-term receivables and other noncurrent assets	1,767	1,801
Deferred income tax charges	88	196
Total Assets	$14,212	$14,370
Liabilities and Shareholders' Equity		
Current Liabilities		
Payables	$ 3,275	$ 3,832
Short-term borrowings	2,206	1,163
Taxes—income and other	572	612
Dividends payable	128	139
Deferred income tax credits	34	23
Total current liabilities	6,215	5,769
Other Liabilities		
Long-term borrowings	1,166	936
Postemployment liabilities	2,610	2,776
Other long-term liabilities	732	918
Deferred income tax credits	61	59
Total Liabilities	10,784	10,458
Shareholders' Equity		
Common stock, par value $2.50 per share 950,000,000 shares authorized;		
issued 391,292,760 shares in 2000 and 1999	978	978
Additional paid in capital	871	889
Retained earnings	7,869	6,995
Accumulated other comprehensive loss	(482)	(145)
	9,236	8,717
Treasury stock, at cost 100,808,494 shares in 2000 and 80,871,830 shares in 1999	5,808	4,805
Total Shareholders' Equity	3,428	3,912
Total Liabilities and Shareholders' Equity	$14,212	$14,370

The accompanying notes are an integral part of these financial statements.

Assets

Current Assets

Assets are separated on a statement of financial condition according to how they are used in the firm's operations. Current assets include cash, cash equivalents, and other assets that are expected to be converted into cash within 1 year or one **operating cycle,** if the operating cycle is longer than 1 year. (An operating cycle is the time required to purchase or manufacture products, sell the goods, and collect the cash.) Current refers to those assets that are in essence used up and replenished in the ongoing business operations. The term **working capital** or net working capital is used© to designate the amount by which current assets exceed current liabilities.

Cash and Cash Equivalents

Cash is cash in any form—cash awaiting deposit or cash on deposit. Cash equivalents are short-term, highly liquid investments that are readily convertible into cash. Kodak's note on its cash equivalents reads, "All highly liquid investments with an original maturity of 3 months or less at date of purchase are considered to be cash equivalents."

Marketable Securities

Marketable securities are short-term investments made to earn a return on cash not needed immediately for business operations. The valuation of marketable securities on the balance sheet as well as other debt and equity securities depends upon the intent of the investment. Kodak's investments in the current asset section are classified as "held to maturity," which means the company has the intent to hold the securities until the maturity date, and they are carried at amortized cost.[2]

Receivables

Receivables or **accounts receivable** are the customer balances outstanding on credit sales. They are reported on the statement of financial condition at their net realizable value, which is the actual amount of the receivables less an allowance for a portion of receivables that management estimates will not be collectable. This estimate is based on factors such as past experience, knowledge of customer quality, the state of the economy, and the company's collection policies. Any actual losses are written off against the allowance account, which is adjusted at the end of the accounting period. The estimation of the allowance account affects both the valuation of receivables on the balance sheet and the recognition of bad debt expense on the earnings statement.

---

[2]   Statement of Financial Accounting Standards No. 115, "Accounting for Certain Investments in Debt and Equity Securities," requires the separation of investment securities into three categories: (1) held to maturity, (2) trading securities, and (3) securities available for sale. Held to maturity are reported at amortized cost; amortized cost refers to the fact that a debt security may sell at a premium or discount because the stated rate of interest differs from the market rate of interest; the premium or discount is amortized over the life of the security, but at maturity, cost equals the face amount. Trading securities are reported at fair value with unrealized gains and losses included in earnings. Securities available for sale are carried at fair value with unrealized gains and losses included in comprehensive income. This accounting requirement significantly affects companies such as financial institutions and insurance companies, which trade heavily in securities as part of their operating activities.

The allowance account can be important in assessing a firm's earnings quality. Generally, there should be a consistent relationship between the rate of change in sales, accounts receivable, and the allowance account; if these amounts are changing at very different rates or moving in opposite directions, a caution flag is raised. Inadequate provision for bad debt expense has been one of the causes of earnings overstatements. Many companies show the allowance amount on the face of the statement of financial condition, but Kodak discloses this information in a financial statement note:

(in millions)	2000	1999
Trade receivables	$2,245	2,140
Miscellaneous receivables	408	397
Total (net of allowances of $89 and $136)	$2,653	2,537

Source: Eastman Kodak Annual Report 2000, from Note 2: "Receivables."

The note states, "Adequate provisions have been recorded for uncollectible receivables. There are no significant concentrations of credit risk."

Have you read enough of this book yet to be skeptical? Let's look at this information another way. Receivables in the financial statement are shown "net" of the allowance account. To determine the total, the allowance amount is added to the net amount shown in the financial statement:

(in millions)	2000	1999
Receivables (from statement of financial position)	$ 2,653	2,537
Allowance (from Note 2)	89	136
Total receivables	$ 2,742	2,673
Sales (from the earnings statement)	13,994	14,089

Total receivables have *increased* from $2,673 million to $2,742 million (3 percent) between 1999 and 2000; but the allowance has *decreased* from $136 million to $89 million (35 percent). From the earnings statement in Chapter 2, we find that Kodak's sales have also *decreased,* from $14,089 million in 1999 to $13,994 (1 percent) in 2000. So now, two caution flags are waving: sales and receivables as well as receivables and the allowance for doubtful accounts are moving in opposite directions.

This is a company that had a miniscule—$15 million (after tax)—growth in earnings for 2000, and now we find that Kodak *reduced* its allowance account by $47 million in spite of *growth* in receivables. That decision alone could have more than provided the earnings gain. Perhaps the declining stock price (from a high of $68 per share in the first quarter to a low of $35 per share in the fourth quarter) indicates that someone else is reading these notes as well.

Inventories

Inventories are items held for sale or used in the manufacture of products that will be sold. A retail company lists only one type of inventory, merchandise inventories purchased for resale to the public; but a company like Kodak, that also manufactures products, carries three categories of inventory: raw materials, work in process, and finished goods:

(in millions)	2000	1999
At FIFO or average cost (approximates current cost)		
Finished goods	$1,155	1,026
Work in process	423	487
Raw materials and supplies	589	471
	$2,167	1,984
LIFO reserve	(449)	(465)
Total	$1,718	1,519

Inventories valued on the LIFO method are approximately 47 percent and 48 percent of total inventories in 2000 and 1999, respectively.

Source: Eastman Kodak Annual Report 2000, from Note 3: "Inventories."

Several issues emerge from this presentation of Kodak's inventory account. The fact that finished goods are growing while work in process is declining could indicate a buildup of unsold goods and accompanying cutbacks in manufacturing.

Note also that Kodak's overall inventories are expanding, while sales are declining:

(in millions)	2000	1999
Sales (from statement of earnings)	$13,994	14,089
Inventories (from statement of financial position)	1,718	1,519

This is a caution flag that has already been discussed, possibly indicating the firm has too much inventory or inventory that is not selling.

Given the relative magnitude of inventory, the method used to value inventory and measure cost of goods sold has considerable impact on the company's reported financial condition and performance. As discussed in Chapter 2, cost of goods sold is based on an assumption about the flow of goods for cost/value purposes. The three cost flow assumptions most frequently used are **last in, first out (LIFO); first in, first out (FIFO); and average cost**— Kodak uses all three. LIFO best matches current costs with current revenue on the income statement; however, during a period of inflation, balance sheet inventory is undervalued, and during deflation inventory is overvalued. FIFO, on the other hand, values balance sheet inventory closer to current cost but understates cost of goods sold on the income statement during inflation and overstates cost of goods sold expense during periods of deflation. Unlike depreciation methods, a company must use the same method for both reporting and tax purposes, if LIFO is chosen for tax purposes, and many companies have switched to LIFO during inflationary periods to benefit from higher cost of goods sold deductions and thus lower tax expense.

When a firm uses LIFO to account for some or all of its inventory, a portion of the inventory on the balance sheet reflects "low, old" costs, making comparison among firms difficult. To deal with this problem, the SEC requires companies to disclose the difference between FIFO and LIFO inventory costs, shown as a **LIFO reserve.** What that means for Kodak is that inventory would be $449 million higher in 2000 and $465 million higher in 1999 if FIFO were used.

Kodak uses the designation "approximates current cost," reflecting the accounting convention of conservatism. If the actual market value of inventory falls below cost, as determined by the cost flow assumption, inventory is written down to market price. The carrying value is never written up. Significant write-downs of inventory

Exhibit 3-2

Eastman Kodak Company
Common Size Balance Sheets

	(PERCENT)				
	2000	1999	1998	1997	1996
Assets					
Current Assets					
Cash & cash equivalents	1.7	2.6	3.1	5.5	12.3
Marketable securities	0.0	0.1	0.3	0.2	0.1
Receivables	18.7	17.7	17.1	17.3	19.0
Inventories	12.1	10.6	9.7	9.5	10.9
Deferred income tax charges	4.0	4.8	5.8	7.3	4.5
Other	2.1	2.1	2.0	1.8	1.4
Total current assets	38.6	37.9	38.0	41.6	48.2
Properties					
Land, buildings and equipment, at cost	91.2	92.5	91.5	97.6	87.2
Less: Accumulated depreciation	(49.6)	(51.1)	(51.4)	(55.7)	(49.6)
Net properties	41.6	41.4	40.1	41.9	37.6
Other Assets					
Goodwill (net of accumulated amortization)	6.7	6.8	8.4	4.2	4.0
Long-term receivables and other noncurrent assets	12.5	12.5	11.6	9.4	8.6
Deferred income tax charges	0.6	1.4	1.9	2.9	1.6
Total Assets	*100.0*	*100.0*	*100.0*	*100.0*	*100.0*

are relatively infrequent. Should a write-down occur, however, it is important to assess the reasons. Possible explanations include an economic recession, an unexpected surge in product supplies, or poor inventory management. In January 2002, for example, Ford Motor Company announced a $1 billion write-down due to the drop in value of the metal palladium used in auto manufacturing.[3] Ford's management made decisions differently from other automobile manufacturers, choosing to stockpile metal as prices rose.

An interesting observation about Kodak's management of assets is found on the common size balance sheet shown in Exhibit 3-2. Similar conceptually to the common size income statement in Chapter 2, the common size balance sheet facilitates structural and trend analysis by expressing all items as a percentage of total assets. Note that Kodak's cash and cash equivalents comprised more than 12 percent of total

---

[3] Gregory L. White, "How Ford's Big Batch of Rare Metal Led to $1 Billion Write Off," *The Wall Street Journal* (February 6, 2002), pp. A1, A6.

Exhibit 3-2
(Continued)

	(PERCENT)				
	2000	1999	1998	1997	1996
Liabilities and Shareholders' Equity					
Current Liabilities					
Payables	23.1	26.7	26.5	29.2	28.5
Short-term borrowings	15.5	8.1	10.3	4.6	3.7
Taxes-income and other	4.0	4.2	4.0	4.3	4.2
Dividends payable	0.9	1.0	1.0	1.1	0.9
Deferred income tax credits	0.2	0.2	0.1	0.2	0.2
Total current liabilities	43.7	40.2	41.9	39.4	37.5
Other Liabilities					
Long-term borrowings	8.2	6.5	3.4	4.5	3.9
Postemployment liabilities	18.4	19.3	20.1	23.4	20.5
Other long-term liabilities	5.2	6.4	7.0	8.2	4.6
Deferred income tax credits	0.4	0.4	0.5	0.5	0.7
Total liabilities	75.9	72.8	72.9	76.0	67.2
Shareholders' Equity					
Common stock	6.9	6.8	6.6	7.4	6.8
Additional paid in capital	6.1	6.2	6.1	7.0	6.3
Retained earnings	55.4	48.7	41.8	40.6	41.1
Accumulated other comprehensive loss	(3.4)	(1.0)	(0.7)	(1.5)	0.5
	65.0	60.7	53.8	53.5	54.7
Treasury stock, at cost	(40.9)	(33.5)	(26.7)	(29.5)	(21.9)
Total shareholders' equity	24.1	27.2	27.1	24.0	32.8
Total Liabilities and Shareholders' Equity	100.0	100.0	100.0	100.0	100.0

assets in 1996. These funds have shifted into such assets as inventory, property, goodwill, long-term receivables, and other noncurrent assets.

Deferred Income Taxes

Deferred taxes (Box 3-1) are the result of **temporary differences** in the recognition of revenue and expense for taxable income relative to reported income. Most companies legitimately use one set of rules for tax purposes and another for preparing financial statements because the objectives are different: firms want to minimize tax payments but maximize or smooth reported profits. There are many areas in which firms are permitted to use different methods, such as depreciation expense, which was discussed in Chapter 2. Other temporary differences arise from accounting for installment sales,

BOX 3-1
Accounting for Deferred Taxes

Deferred tax accounts reconcile temporary differences in expense and revenue recognition for the accounting period. Deferred taxes are classified as current or noncurrent depending upon the underlying temporary difference: a difference relating to 90-day warranties would be considered current, but one for 5-year warranties would be noncurrent.

The deferred tax is a liability when the item causes reported income to exceed taxable income with the expectation that the difference would be offset in future periods. Deferred tax assets are reported for operating loss and tax credit carryforwards and for deductible temporary differences that cause taxable income to exceed reported income, with the expectation that the difference will be offset in the future.

long-term contracts, leases, warranties and service contracts, pensions and other employment benefits, and subsidiary investment earnings.

They are called temporary differences (or timing differences) because, in theory, the total amount of expense and revenue recognized will eventually be the same for tax and reporting purposes. There are also **permanent differences** in tax accounting; municipal bond revenue, for example, is recognized as income for reporting purposes but not for tax. Permanent differences do not affect deferred taxes.

Kodak is an interesting example because it shows deferred taxes in all four categories of its statement of financial position: current asset, noncurrent asset, current liability, and noncurrent liability. The items giving rise to the deferrals are disclosed in Note 10, "Income Taxes." Deferred tax assets are the result of postemployment obligations, restructuring programs, inventories, and tax loss carryforwards; liabilities arise from depreciation, leasing, and other unspecified items. Deferred tax assets are listed as "charges" and liabilities as "credits." Overall, Kodak has net deferred tax assets of $568 and $803 million, respectively, in 2000 and 1999.[4] What this means is that, in future years, it is probable that Kodak will actually pay less in taxes than what is reported as tax expense on the income statement.

Other Current Assets
Most companies have certain expenses such as insurance, rent, property taxes, and utilities that are sometimes paid in advance. There is no explanation provided in Kodak's notes about its other current assets, but they probably include such prepaid items.

Properties
This category encompasses Kodak's tangible, long-lived assets (also called fixed assets or capital assets) that are not used up in the ebb and flow of annual business operations. Such assets produce economic benefits for more than 1 year, and they are considered tangible because they have physical substance. The cost of these assets, with the exception of land which is assumed to have an unlimited useful life, is allocated over the period they will benefit the firm, through the process of depreciation. The carrying value on the statement of financial condition is cost less accumulated depreciation to date.

---

[4] These numbers were obtained by adding the two deferred income tax charges on the statement of financial condition and subtracting the two deferred income tax credits.

The relative proportion of capital assets in a firm's asset structure will depend on the nature of the business. A firm, like Kodak, that manufactures products will be more capital intensive than a company that is exclusively a retailer or wholesaler. The absolute amount of Kodak's investment in capital assets decreased slightly between 1999 and 2000. But the common size balance sheet shown in Exhibit 3-2 reveals that Kodak's capital assets comprise almost 42 percent of total assets, modestly increasing in proportion over the last 5 years.

Goodwill

Goodwill arises when one company acquires another company and pays more than the fair market value of its net identifiable assets (identifiable assets less liabilities assumed). This excess price is recorded on the balance sheet as goodwill. Kodak's goodwill account is shown net of accumulated amortization.

Background on Accounting for Goodwill. Prior to the issuance of FASB Statement No. 142, "Goodwill and Other Intangible Assets," there were two methods of accounting for acquisitions: pooling (financial statements combined and no goodwill recognized) and purchase (creation of goodwill for amount in excess of net identifiable assets). Under the purchase method, goodwill is shown as an asset on the balance sheet, and the cost "amortized" over a period not to exceed 40 years. As of January 1, 2002, the FASB eliminated the pooling method entirely, and goodwill under the purchase method will no longer be amortized. Beginning in 2002, companies will evaluate goodwill and determine whether it has lost value. If it has, the amount of impairment will be expensed in the year the determination is made. No write-up is recorded for gains. What that means is that some corporations will take enormous write-offs when companies they have acquired have lost value. As implementation of this new rule takes place, earnings may increase for some firms relative to prior years because amortization expense will no longer be recorded—the increased earnings reflect a "paper" increase due to the FASB rule change. Companies will also have some discretion in deciding when and how much write-off to take as a result of goodwill impairment.

In a study of the 1,000 largest U.S. companies conducted by *Business Week* and Standard & Poor's in 2001, it was estimated that dozens of companies would have multimillion dollar goodwill write-offs.[5] Qwest, for example, has announced that its 2002 write-off will be $30–40 billion, arising largely from the acquisition of U.S. West. On the plus side, firms will not have to deduct amortization expense each year, which will increase earnings for many companies. Kodak has estimated that in 2002, the year the rule becomes effective, not having to deduct amortization expense will boost earnings by 45 cents per share.

Long-Term Receivables and Other Noncurrent Assets

There is no breakdown provided in Kodak's financial statement notes about the long-term receivables and other noncurrent assets account. Long-term receivables apply to accounts that are due after 1 year or one operating cycle. Other noncurrent

---

5   Peter Elstrom, David Henry, David Welch, and Stephanie Anderson, "Today, Nortel. Tomorrow . . .," *Business Week* (July 2, 2001), pp. 32–35.

assets can include a multitude of items such as property held for sale, start-up costs in connection with new businesses, the cash surrender value of life insurance policies, and long-term advance payments. This account is certainly important to Kodak's financial condition because it is larger than inventories and (as shown in Exhibit 3-2) now represents 12.5 percent of the company's assets. A caution flag is raised because the reader of Kodak's report has not been provided with information about the components of this account.[6]

Total Assets

Total assets for Kodak have actually shrunk slightly, from $14,370 million in 1999, to $14,212 million in 2000. Companies generally want to show productive growth with increases in assets over time. Kodak's reduction in its asset base reflects the restructuring programs and sales of divisions discussed in Chapter 2.

Liabilities

Current Liabilities

Liabilities represent claims against assets. Liabilities designated as current are those that are expected to be satisfied with current assets and within a time frame of 1 year (or one operating cycle, whichever is longer). For example, accounts payable to suppliers, a current liability, is settled with cash, a current asset.

Payables

Accounts payable are short-term obligations that arise from credit extended by suppliers for the purchase of goods and services. When Kodak buys raw materials on credit from a supplier, the transaction creates a payable. This account is eliminated when payment is made. The ongoing process of operating a business results in the spontaneous generation of payables, which increase and decrease depending upon the credit policies of suppliers, economic conditions, and the cyclical nature of the firm's business. Reference to Kodak's common size balance sheet (Exhibit 3-2) shows that this is the largest liability account over the past 5 years, indicating that suppliers provide a significant source of Kodak's credit.

Short-Term Borrowings

Short-term borrowings for most firms typically encompass promissory notes to suppliers or financial institutions. Kodak's note on short-term borrowings indicates that its borrowings included $1,809 million and $894 million of commercial paper (unsecured promissory notes) at year-end 2000 and 1999, respectively. The weighted-average

---

[6]   As an example of why this account is important, Kodak reports in Note 16, "Sales of Assets and Divestitures," that in 1998 the company sold all of its shares of Fox Photo, Inc. to Wolf Camera for an amount approximating the current value of Fox Photo's net assets. There is no other information about that sale. But in June 2001 Wolf Camera filed for bankruptcy protection with Kodak listed as one of its creditors. Whatever amount Wolf owed Kodak, the collection of which is now questionable, may have been carried in this account by Kodak in 1999 and 2000, but there is no way to determine what that amount is or the source of the other long-term receivables. In 2001, Kodak took a $77 million charge relating to the bankruptcy of Wolf Camera and a $20 million charge associated with the Kmart bankruptcy.

interest rate of borrowings outstanding at year end was 6.4 percent in 2000 and 5.8 percent in 1999.

Kodak's short-term borrowings almost doubled in 2000. In spite of an overall reduction in its asset base, Kodak's inventories and receivables have grown, but not as much as short-term borrowing. Kodak's borrowing needs reflect the fact that its cash flow from operations, as discussed in Chapter 2, fell sharply in 2000.

Taxes and Dividends Payable

Taxes payable represent taxes that have been expensed (per the accrual basis of accounting) but not yet paid. Dividends payable are amounts that have been declared by the company but not yet paid to shareholders.

Long-Term Borrowings

Obligations with maturities beyond 1 year are designated on the statement of financial condition as noncurrent liabilities. This category can include bond indebtedness, long-term notes payable, mortgages, obligations under leases, and long-term warranties. The current portion (due within 1 year) of long-term debt is included in current liabilities.

Long-term borrowings represent an increasing portion of Kodak's liabilities—Note 6, "Long-Term Borrowings," to the Kodak financial statement specifies the nature, maturity, and interest rate of each long-term obligation. The company's long-term borrowings include notes, with interest rates ranging from 5.85 percent to 9.95 percent, debentures (unsecured bonds) with interest rates ranging from 1.98 percent to 3.16 percent, and "other" undefined long-term borrowings with rates ranging from 2.00 percent to 17.00 percent. Kodak's long-term borrowings have risen during a period of reduced net investment in capital assets. As with short-term debt, this borrowing need in part reflects the reductions in cash flow from operations.

The comprehensive analysis of Kodak's long-term solvency in Chapter 5 includes an evaluation of proportion of debt in Kodak's capital structure, its ability to service debt, and its effectiveness in using debt. Debt (Box 3-2) carries risk but it also provides benefits to owners[7] when used effectively.

Postemployment Liabilities

Pension accounting is a major headache for most readers of financial statements and almost all students of accounting. In spite of the complexities, it is important to understand pension accounting, at least in broad terms, because the accounting for pensions can provide a major source of profit or loss.

Most of what you see for Kodak's postemployment liability, however, does not relate to its primary pension funding. Companies are required to report as a balance sheet liability certain postemployment obligations—for example to pay medical bills for retired employees and spouses by accruing promised future benefits, even though the benefits are paid from general company funds as they occur. The liability recorded on Kodak's statement of financial condition primarily reflects obligations under postretirement benefits other than pensions.

---

[7] Shareholder returns are magnified through financial leverage when a firm earns returns on its borrowings greater than its after tax cost of debt.

BOX 3-2
Keeping Debt Off the Books

Many firms use complicated financing schemes—product financing arrangements, sales of receivables with recourse, limited partnerships, joint ventures—that do not have to be recorded on balance sheets. Disclosures about the extent, nature, and terms of **off-balance-sheet financing** arrangements are in the notes to the financial statements, but they may be very complex, difficult to understand, and require putting pieces together from several different sections.

The complicated arrangements that contributed to the demise of Enron are definitely in this complex and hidden-information category. The debt that did not appear on Enron's balance sheet may have been discussed in the notes, but it was very difficult to find and understand.

The following is an example of Enron's description of a potential obligation from its 2000 annual report:

> In connection with the 1998 financial restructuring (yielding proceeds of approximately $1.2 billion) of Enron's investment in Azurix, Enron committed to cause the sale of Enron convertible preferred stock, if certain debt obligations of the related entity which acquired an interest in Azurix, are defaulted upon, or in certain events, including, among other things, Enron's credit ratings fall below specified levels. If the sale of the convertible preferred stock is not sufficient to retire such obligations, Enron would be liable for the shortfall.

This "explanation" is provided in the middle of a note in the middle of pages and pages of complicated notes that are equally difficult to decipher.

A caution flag is justified—at least regarding the quality of an annual report's disclosures—when the explanatory notes to a company's financial statements *obscure* rather than *clarify*. Even as far back as the 1996 annual report, discussed in Chapter 1, it was difficult to understand Enron's explanatory material. As the company's financial dealings intensified in complexity and murkiness, so too did its financial statement notes.

Another useful approach in identifying possible problems with a firm's presentation is to look at the notes over a period of time and determine what changes have been made from one period to the next and what new material has been added. Between its 1997 annual report, with the green leaf on the cover, and its 1998 annual report, with the photos of happy, hard-working employees on the cover, Enron's financial statement note on "unconsolidated subsidiaries" changed to "unconsolidated affiliates"[8] and grew from *8* inches of tables with no explanatory text to *18* inches of tables with a considerable amount of obtuse text. In the 1999 annual report, Enron introduced a new five-paragraph note on "Related Party Transactions" in which the company discloses information about entering a series of new transactions with limited partnerships, and for one of these, a senior officer of Enron is the managing member. (Readers would also need the 1999 proxy statement to discover the "senior officer" was none other than Enron Chief Financial Officer Andrew Fastow who stood to benefit considerably from the partnerships.)[9] With the publication of its 2000 annual report, Enron's "Related Party Transactions" footnote had more than doubled in length and at least quadrupled in complexity.

---

[8] One of the ways Enron kept debt off its books was through the formation of limited partnerships, in which Enron transferred assets to a partnership, moving the assets and liabilities off Enron's balance sheet and recognizing a gain from the transfer. If an outside investor injects 3 percent of partnership capital, FASB rules do not classify the partnership as a subsidiary. "Murky Waters: A Primer on Enron Partnerships," *The Wall Street Journal* (January 21, 2001), p. C1.

[9] Dan Feldstein, "What was bottom line at Enron?" *The Houston Chronicle* (March 18, 2002), p. 1A.

Pension Accounting. U.S. firms have two types of pension plans—defined contribution and defined benefits. An increasing number of companies (now about 50 percent) use **defined contribution** plans, in which the employer specifies the amount contributed to the plan for the employee. The amount that the employee will receive at retirement is not specified, and the employee bears the risk of the plan. A 401(k) plan is a defined contribution plan. The expense recognized by the company is the amount contributed to the plan.

The accounting for a **defined benefit** plan, used by Kodak, is much more complicated.[10] These plans specify the amount that will be paid to employees after retirement, which requires measuring the liability—a difficult process involving estimations in the length of employees' service, the increase in salary levels over time, the length of time benefits will be paid, and expected interest rates. To offset the liability, the company has pension assets, which incorporate a smoothing mechanism to eliminate some of the effect of swings in the stock market. The smoothing mechanism takes into account market values for several years rather than just the current year.

Neither the fair value of pension plan assets nor the projected benefit obligation appear on the balance sheet of the company, but rather are disclosed in notes. The net amount of the pension asset and obligation does appear in the balance sheet but may be combined in an "other" account. The funding status is important, however, because the company is ultimately responsible for any underfunded amount—that is, if pension obligations exceed pension assets.

Kodak has pension plans both in the United States and abroad. Kodak's plans are overfunded at year-end 2000, which means that its pension assets exceed its pension obligations. Although Kodak does not clearly specify this information on the statement of financial condition, it is probably included in "other noncurrent assets":

(in millions)	U.S.	Non-U.S.
Projected benefit obligation at December 31, 2000	$5,530	1,761
Fair value of plan assets at December 31, 2000	7,290	1,880

Source: Eastman Kodak Annual Report 2000, from Note 12: "Retirement Plans."

The amount that does directly affect the company's earnings statement is the **annual pension cost or income** recognized, which is based on an extremely complicated series of accounting measurements. This explanation is simplified, but each year the company estimates the cost of pension benefits and the expected return on pension assets. If the expected return exceeds the cost, the company recognizes income; if the return is less, the difference is an expense.

Many companies have benefited from the bull market of the 1990s with large boosts to earnings from their pension plans because the expected returns have exceeded the costs.[11] That situation reverses when values decline, even though the effect of falling returns in a bear market is not felt immediately because of the smoothing feature. Income may continue to rise for a time, but eventually a reversal

---

[10] Helpful articles on this topic are David Henry, "Why Earnings Are Too Rosy," *Business Week* (August 13, 2001), pp. 68–69; and Anne Tergesen, "The Fine Print: How to Read Those Key Footnotes," *Business Week* (February 4, 2002), pp. 94–96.

[11] Some of the gains are enormous; in 2000, the increase in earnings from pension plans for General Electric was over $1 billion and for IBM more than $800 million.

will occur and have a negative impact on earnings. The disclosures relating to annual pension expense or income are also found in the financial statement notes.[12]

For 2000, Kodak recognized net pension income of $95 million in the United States but pension expense of $64 million for non-U.S. plans, resulting in $31 million net pension income. That amount is included in Kodak's net earnings for 2000:

	2000	
(in millions)	U.S.	Non-U.S.
Service cost	$ 89	33
Interest cost	408	107
Expected return on plan assets	(572)	(147)
Amortization of:		
Transition asset	(59)	(10)
Prior service cost	1	8
Actuarial loss	—	3
Curtailments	(3)	—
Settlements	—	1
Net pension (income) expense	(136)	(5)
Other plans including unfunded plans	41	69
Total net pension (income) expense	$ (95)	64

Source: Eastman Kodak Annual Report 2000, from Note 12: "Retirement Plans."

Other Long-Term Liabilities

The "other long-term liabilities" account for Kodak includes deferred compensation (employee compensation that has been expensed but not yet paid) and minority interest in Kodak companies. **Minority interest** arises because Kodak prepares consolidated financial statements for investments in other companies of more than 50 percent; the minority interest reflects the portion of ownership that is not owned by Kodak (a discussion of accounting for such investments is provided in Chapter 2). Many companies report minority interest as a separate item on the statement of financial condition.

The remaining portion of Kodak's other long-term liabilities account is not explained in the note on other long-term liabilities:

---

[12] Companies with defined benefit plans disclose the following: (1) a description of the plan, including employee groups covered, type of benefit formula, funding policy, and types of assets held; (2) the amount of pension expense showing separately the service cost component, the interest cost component, the actual return on assets for the period, and the net total of other components; (3) a schedule reconciling the funded status of the plan with amounts reported on the balance sheet; (4) the weighted average discount rate and rate of compensation increase used to measure the projected benefit obligation and the weighted average expected long-term rate of return on plan assets; and (5) the amounts and types of securities included in plan assets.

The service cost represents the increase during the year in the discounted present value of payable benefits, resulting from employees' working an additional year. Interest cost arises from the passage of time and increases interest expense. Return on plan assets reduces pension expense; other components include net amortization and deferrals and are related to the choice of discount and interest rates. The same rate must be used to compute service cost and interest cost, but a different rate can be used to compute the expected rate of return on pension plan assets.

(in millions)	2000	1999
Deferred compensation	$146	160
Minority interest in Kodak companies	93	98
Other	493	660
Total	$732	918

Source: Eastman Kodak Annual Report 2000, from Note 7: "Other Long-Term Liabilities."

As shown in the note, the largest portion of this account is simply labeled "other." Again, this is a problem because there is no way of determining from the note the nature of Kodak's obligations. According to Note 8 in Kodak's annual report, the company has environmental remediation costs that have been accrued as liabilities because they have not yet been paid. It is possible that these accrued liabilities are part of the "Other" account.

Commitments and Contingencies

Commitments refer to contractual agreements that will have a significant impact on the company in the future. Operating leases (Box 3-3) are a form of off-balance-sheet financing, and these commitments must be disclosed in notes to the financial statements. **Contingencies** are potential liabilities of the firm such as possible damage awards assessed in lawsuits. Generally, the firm cannot reasonably predict the outcome and/or the amount of the future liability, but information must be disclosed.

Companies discuss commitments and contingencies in financial statement notes and are required by the SEC to show a caption on the balance sheet, "Commitments

BOX 3-3
Accounting for Leases

Leases are another area of corporate operations that can be extremely complicated but have a significant impact on the firm's reported financial condition. The FASB's rule on leasing, Statement No.13, "Accounting for Leases," was issued in part to require companies to put certain kinds of leasing arrangements (that were in essence purchases financed by debt) on their financial statements. There are two kinds of leases: operating and capital.

An **operating lease** is a conventional rental agreement with no ownership rights transferring to the lessee at the end of the rental contract. A **capital lease** is a leasing arrangement which is, in substance, a purchase rather than a lease. If a lease meets any one of four criteria—transfers ownership to the lessee, contains a bargain purchase option, has a lease term of 75 percent or more of the leased property's economic life, or has minimum lease payments with a present value of 90 percent or more of the property's fair value—the lease must be recorded as a capital lease.

Both the balance sheet and the income statement are affected by a capital lease. An asset and liability are recorded on the lessee's balance sheet, reflecting what is, in essence, the purchase of an asset; the liability is the obligation incurred in financing the purchase. Each lease payment is apportioned partly to reduce the outstanding liability and partly to interest expense. The asset account is amortized with amortization expense recognized on the income statement, just as a purchased asset would be depreciated.

and Contingencies," even though no dollar amount appears.[13] This disclosure is intended to draw attention to the fact that required information can be found in the notes to the financial statements. Kodak, which has a lengthy discussion of commitments and contingencies in a financial statement note, has not complied with this SEC rule to provide the balance sheet caption.

Kodak's Note 8 discloses the firm's "Commitments and Contingencies." These involve projected increases in expenditures for pollution prevention and waste treatment, a compliance schedule relating to a suit brought by the U.S. Environmental Protection Agency and Justice Department, several environmental actions, expenditures relating to the Clean Air Act, agreements with companies that provide Kodak with products and services, operating leases, and guaranteed debt under agreements with affiliated companies. Kodak has known and estimated commitments totaling $1,668 million according to its note, including operating leases of $351 million.

Total Liabilities

Total liabilities for Kodak rose very slightly between 1999 and 2000. Since the asset base decreased, the proportion of overall debt has risen. Kodak's common sized balance sheet, Exhibit 3-2, reflects this increase, with liabilities as a proportion of total assets growing from 72.8 percent to 75.9 percent. As discussed earlier, most of the growth in liabilities is the result of increased borrowings.

Hybrid Securities

Some companies have **mandatorily redeemable preferred stock** outstanding. Kodak does not issue these securities, but they are explained here because they have the characteristics of both debt and equity. The financial instrument is called preferred stock (see discussion in the equity section), but the issuing company must retire the shares at a future date, so it is actually debt. Any preferred stock with a mandatory redemption is shown between the liabilities and equity section of the statement of financial condition.

Shareholders' Equity

The ownership interests in the company are represented in the shareholders' or stockholders' equity section of the statement of financial condition. Ownership equity is the residual interest in assets that would remain after satisfying all of the liabilities.

Common Stock and Additional Paid in Capital

Kodak has only common stock shares outstanding. Common shareholders do not ordinarily receive a fixed return but do have voting privileges in proportion to ownership interest. Dividends on common stock are declared at the discretion of the company's board of directors. Some companies also issue **preferred stock**, which usually carries a fixed annual dividend payment but no voting rights.

The amount listed in the **common stock** account is based on the par or stated value of the shares issued. The **par or stated value** bears no relationship to the actual

---

[13] Securities and Exchange Commission, S-X Rule 5-02.25.

market price but rather is a floor price below which the shares cannot be initially sold. Kodak's par value is $2.50 per share. The additional paid in capital account reflects the amount by which the original sales price of Kodak's shares exceeded par value. For example, if Kodak sells 100 shares of $2.50 par value stock for $7.50 per share, the common stock account increases $250 (100 × 2.50) and the additional paid in capital $500 (100 × 5.00). This account also bears no relationship to the current market price of the stock.

Retained Earnings

At the end of every accounting period revenues and expenses are tallied, and the difference is net earnings or profit. The retained earnings account is the sum of all the company's profits since it began operations, less any payments made to shareholders in the form of cash or stock dividends. Retained earnings are *not* piles of unused cash stashed away in vaults and should not be confused with cash. Rather, these are the earnings that have not been distributed to shareholders but reinvested in the firm's ongoing business operations.

Accumulated Other Comprehensive Loss

When net earnings are measured at the end of the accounting period, there are some items that are "like" a revenue or expense but are not treated in the same way. They are "unrealized gains and losses" so the accounting rules do not require them to be counted as part of earnings on the income statement. Instead, the changes go directly to equity, where they are "accumulated" in a separate account. **Accumulated other comprehensive income or loss** may include: (1) unrealized gains or losses in the market value of investments in marketable securities classified as available for sale; (2) a specific type of pension liability adjustment; (3) certain gains and losses on derivative financial instruments;[14] and (4) foreign currency translation adjustments resulting when financial statements from a foreign currency are converted into U.S. dollars.

Kodak has an accumulated other comprehensive loss of $482 million at year-end 2000. The components of this account are shown in the statement of shareholders' equity. The largest portion of its accumulated comprehensive loss is the result of foreign currency translation adjustments.

Treasury Stock

Companies often repurchase their own shares for a variety of reasons that include meeting requirements for employee stock option and retirement plans, building shareholdings for prospective mergers, increasing earnings per share by reducing the number of shares outstanding, preventing takeover attempts by reducing the number of shareholders, and investing excess cash holdings. If the repurchased shares are not retired, they are designated as treasury stock and are shown as an offsetting account in the shareholders' equity section.[15] At year-end 2000, Kodak had over 100 million shares in treasury stock at a cost of $5,808 million.

---

14 Financial instruments, such as forward contracts, derive their value from an underlying asset or index.

15 The two methods used to account for treasury stock are the cost method (deducting the cost of the purchased shares from equity) and the par value method (deducting the par or stated value of the shares from equity). Most companies use the cost method.

Stock Options.   One of the uses of treasury stock is for employee stock option plans, which have become an increasingly important source of employee compensation, especially for top managers. The advantage to companies of using stock options is that, unlike conventional payments of salaries, the cost of options does not have to be recognized as a deduction from earnings.[16] Options give the holder the right to purchase company shares at a stated price by a certain date. If the market price rises above that amount, the employee exercises the option and makes a profit. The difference between the option price and the market price is deductible for tax purposes; companies with large numbers of options exercised at wide price differentials in a given year may pay little or no income tax as a result.

Even though there is no expense reported on the published earnings statement, there is a cost, and the cost is carried by shareholders. First, individual shareholder earnings are diluted because when the options are exercised there are more shares outstanding. Second, shareholders lose because the company is selling its shares below the current market price that would otherwise generate relatively more capital for the company to use productively.

Information about employee stock options is disclosed in the firm's proxy statement and in financial statement notes. The accounting rules[17] require that companies show what net income would have been if compensation expense had been recognized for the fair value of its stock options. Kodak reported (in Note 14, "Stock Options and Compensation Plans") 44.8 million shares under option at the end of 2000 with a price range of $32.50 to $92.31 per share. Options for 1.3 million shares were exercised during 2000 ranging from $30.25 to $58.63 per share. If Kodak had recognized compensation expense for stock options, its earnings would have dropped from $1,407 to $1,346 million.

STATEMENT OF SHAREHOLDERS' EQUITY

Although the statement of shareholders' equity is not widely used for analysis and will not be covered in detail, it is included here as one of the four required financial statements. The statement of shareholders' equity provides specific information about reasons for the changes in each of the accounts from the shareholders' equity section of a balance sheet for a 3-year period. Kodak's "Statement of Shareholders' Equity" is presented in Exhibit 3-3.

Kodak's equity accounts are listed across the top of the statement: common stock, additional paid in capital, retained earnings, accumulated other comprehensive income (loss), treasury stock, and total. For 1998, 1999, and 2000, the statement listed the beginning balance in each account and traced through the changes in that account to its ending balance, which becomes the beginning balance for the following year.

---

[16]   For more reading on this topic see Justin Fox, "The amazing stock option sleight of hand," *Fortune* (June 25, 2001), pp. 86–92.

[17]   Statement of Financial Accounting Standards, No. 123, "Accounting for Stock-Based Compensation."

Exhibit 3-3
Eastman Kodak Company and Subsidiary Companies
Consolidated Statement of Shareholders' Equity

(In millions, except number of shares)	Common Stock*	Additional Paid in Capital	Retained Earnings	Accumulated Other Comprehensive Income (Loss)	Treasury Stock	Total
Shareholders' Equity December 31, 1997	$ 978	$ 914	$ 5,343	$ (202)	$ (3,872)	$ 3,161
Net earnings	—	—	1,390	—	—	1,390
Other comprehensive income (loss):						
Unrealized holding gains arising during the period ($122 million pre-tax)	—	—	—	—	—	80
Reclassification adjustment for gains included in net earnings ($86 million pre-tax)	—	—	—	—	—	(44)
Currency translation adjustments	—	—	—	—	—	59
Minimum pension liability adjustment ($7 million pre-tax)	—	—	—	—	—	(4)
Other comprehensive income	—	—	—	91	—	91
Comprehensive income	—	—	—	—	—	1,481
Cash dividends declared	—	—	(570)	—	—	(570)
Treasury stock repurchased (3,541,295 shares)	—	—	—	—	(258)	(258)
Treasury stock issued under employee plans (3,272,713 shares)	—	(58)	—	—	186	128
Tax reductions—employee plans	—	46	—	—	—	46
Shareholders' Equity December 31, 1998	978	902	6,163	(111)	(3,944)	3,988
Net earnings	—	—	1,392	—	—	1,392
Other comprehensive income (loss):						
Unrealized holding gains arising during the period ($115 million pre-tax)	—	—	—	—	—	83
Reclassification adjustment for gains included in net earnings ($20 million pre-tax)	—	—	—	—	—	(13)
Currency translation adjustments	—	—	—	—	—	(118)
Minimum pension liability adjustment ($26 million pre-tax)	—	—	—	—	—	14
Other comprehensive loss	—	—	—	(34)	—	(34)
Comprehensive income	—	—	—	—	—	1,358
Cash dividends declared	—	—	(560)	—	—	(560)
Treasury stock repurchased (13,482,648 shares)	—	—	—	—	(925)	(925)
Treasury stock issued under employee plans (1,105,220 shares)	—	(24)	—	—	64	40
Tax reductions—employee plans	—	11	—	—	—	11
Shareholders' Equity December 31, 1999	978	889	6,995	(145)	(4,805)	3,912
Net earnings	—	—	1,407	—	—	1,407
Other comprehensive income (loss)						
Unrealized holding loss arising during the period ($77 million pre-tax)	—	—	—	—	—	(48)
Reclassification adjustment for gains included in net earnings ($94 million pre-tax)	—	—	—	—	—	(58)
Unrealized loss arising from hedging activity ($55 million pre-tax)	—	—	—	—	—	(34)
Reclassification adjustment for hedging related gains included in net earnings ($6 million pre-tax)	—	—	—	—	—	(4)
Currency translation adjustments	—	—	—	—	—	(194)
Minimum pension liability adjustment ($2 million pre-tax)	—	—	—	—	—	1
Other comprehensive loss	—	—	—	(337)	—	(337)
Comprehensive income	—	—	—	—	—	1,070
Cash dividends declared	—	—	(533)	—	—	(533)
Treasury stock repurchased (21,575,536 shares)	—	—	—	—	(1,099)	(1,099)
Treasury stock issued under employee plans (1,638,872 shares)	—	(33)	—	—	96	63
Tax reductions—employee plans	—	15	—	—	—	15
Shareholders' Equity December 31, 2000	$ 978	$ 871	$ 7,869	$ (482)	$ (5,808)	$ 3,428

*There are 100 million shares of $10 par value preferred stock authorized, none of which have been issued.

Accumulated unrealized holding gains, related to available for sale securities, as of December 31, 2000, 1999, and 1998 were $7 million, $113 million, and $43 million respectively. Accumulated unrealized losses related to hedging activity as of December 31, 2000 were $(38). Accumulated translation adjustments as of December 31, 2000, 1999, and 1998 were $(425) million, $(231) million, and $(113) million, respectively. Accumulated minimum pension liability adjustments as of December 31, 2000, 1999, and 1998 were $(26) million, $(27) million, and $(41) million, respectively.

The accompanying notes are an integral part of these financial statements.

BOX 3-4
Stock Dividends and Stock Splits

Some companies have **stock dividends** or **stock splits** during an accounting period. With stock dividends, the company issues to existing shareholders additional shares of stock in proportion to current ownership. Stock dividends reduce the retained earnings account.[18] Unlike a cash dividend that results in the receipt of cash, a stock dividend represents nothing of value to the shareholder. The shareholder has more shares, but the proportion of ownership is exactly the same, and the company's net assets (assets minus liabilities) are exactly the same. The market value of the stock should drop in proportion to the additional shares issued.

Stock splits also result in the issuance of additional shares in proportion to current ownership and represent nothing of value to the shareholder; they are generally used to lower the market price of a firm's shares. For example, if a company declares a 2 for 1 stock split, a shareholder with 100 shares ends up with 200 shares, and the market price of the stock should fall by 50 percent. The company makes no accounting entry but does have a memorandum item noting the change in the par value of the stock and the change in the number of shares outstanding.

As an example of what this statement shows, Kodak's retained earnings account records increases each of the 3 years with the addition of net earnings for the period and decreases as the result of cash dividends. Kodak paid cash dividends in each of the 3 years shown in the statement of shareholders' equity. The amount of dividends paid is $1.76 per common share (Exhibit 1-5), but the amount declined each year because of the reductions through treasury stock purchases in the number of common shares outstanding.

Other comprehensive income has been affected by security holdings, reclassification adjustments,[19] pension liability adjustments, and foreign currency translation adjustments (see "total" column). Kodak's treasury stock account shows the repurchase of shares in each of the 3 years and the issuance of shares under employee plans.

Additional Accounts

Corporate balance sheet and equity statements are not limited to the accounts discussed in this chapter. Readers of annual reports will encounter additional accounts and also find many of the same accounts listed under different titles. Those discussed in this chapter,[20] however, should be sufficient for understanding the basics of most financial statement presentations.

---

[18] The retained earnings account is reduced by the market value of the shares issued for a small stock dividend (less than 20–25 percent of the number of shares outstanding) or by the par value of the stock for a large stock dividend (more than 20–25 percent).

[19] Relating to forward contracts.

[20] Except for specialized industries, such as banks and public utilities.

READERS' CHECKLIST OF CAUTION FLAGS FROM CHAPTER 3

➢ Reductions in the allowance for doubtful accounts when accounts receivable are increasing

➢ Sales and receivables growing at substantially different rates or moving in opposite directions

➢ Sales and inventories growing at substantially different rates or moving in opposite directions

➢ Categories of inventories moving in opposite directions

➢ Excessive use of "other" for material, unexplained items

➢ Write-down in value of goodwill

➢ Borrowings growing faster than assets being financed; debt rising when assets are decreasing

➢ Financial statement notes obscure rather than enlighten

➢ Changes in and additions to financial statement notes require Ph.D. in accounting and measurement by yardstick rather than ruler

➢ Substantial amount of income from unpredictable and possibly unsustainable sources, such as pension plans

➢ Extensive use of stock options for employee compensation

TEST YOURSELF

Solutions are provided immediately following the Glossary at the end of the book.

1. What does a statement of financial condition summarize for a firm?
   a. Net income at a point in time
   b. Revenues, expenses, and equity for a period
   c. What the firm owns and owes
   d. Detailed changes of each equity account

2. What is the balancing equation for the statement of financial condition?
   a. Assets = liabilities + shareholders' equity
   b. Revenues – expenses = net income
   c. Assets = liabilities
   d. Assets + liabilities = shareholders' equity

3. What are current assets?
   a. Assets that are currently being used to make operations more efficient
   b. Assets that are expected to be converted into cash within 1 year or one operating cycle, whichever is longer
   c. Assets that are prepaid
   d. Assets that will be paid within 1 year

4. Which of the following would be classified as current assets?
   a. Intangibles, payables, cash
   b. Inventory, receivables, payables
   c. Buildings, prepaid expenses, treasury stock
   d. Marketable securities, receivables, inventories

5. How can the allowance for doubtful accounts be used to overstate earnings?
   a. The allowance account could be underestimated.
   b. The allowance account could be overestimated.

c. The allowance account could be changed proportionately with sales and accounts receivable.

d. The allowance account cannot be used in any way to impact earnings.

6. During a period of inflation, which inventory method would most likely undervalue the inventory account on the statement of financial condition?

a. FIFO

b. LIFO

c. Average cost

d. Straight-line

7. Which method of inventory best matches current costs with current revenues?

a. FIFO

b. LIFO

c. Average cost

d. Straight-line

8. What causes companies to record deferred income taxes?

a. Permanent differences in tax accounting

b. The inability to pay taxes on time

c. Temporary differences between taxable and reported income caused by using a different set of rules for tax purposes compared to financial reporting purposes

d. Both (a) and (b)

9. Which of the following statements about goodwill is false?

a. Goodwill arises when one company acquires another company and pays more than the fair market value of its net identifiable assets.

b. A new rule just recently issued by FASB requires that all goodwill be written off in 2002.

c. Goodwill under the purchase method will no longer be amortized.

d. Earnings per share will most likely be boosted in 2002 when companies implement FASB's new rule eliminating amortization for goodwill.

10. Which of the following items would be classified as current liabilities?

a. Advertising expense, payables, short-term borrowings

b. Leases, deferred taxes, common stock

c. Payables, short-term borrowings, dividends payable

d. Sales, long-term investments, long-term debt

11. What is off-balance-sheet financing?

a. Financing schemes used to keep debt off the books

b. Offering credit to customers

c. Financing arrangements that often cause accountants to lose their balance

d. Financing schemes that are illegal

12. Which statement is true?

a. A 401(k) plan is a defined benefit pension plan.

b. The accounting for a defined contribution plan is more complicated than a defined benefit pension plan.

c. New economy companies must use defined benefit plans.

d. A defined benefit pension plan specifies the amount that will be paid to employees after retirement.

13. Which statement is false?
    a. The quality of a financial statement is enhanced when a firm uses the "other" account for material items.
    b. When expected returns exceed costs in pension plans, companies may benefit from a large boost to earnings.
    c. Mandatorily redeemable preferred stock has characteristics of both debt and equity.
    d. Important information can be gained by reading the notes related to liabilities.
14. What is the difference between an operating and a capital lease?
    a. A capital lease is a form of off-balance-sheet financing and an operating lease is not.
    b. A capital lease is, in substance, a purchase rather than a lease, and an operating lease is a rental agreement.
    c. An operating lease transfers ownership to the lessee, whereas a capital lease contains a bargain purchase option.
    d. An operating lease is used in operations and a capital lease is used for financing.
15. Why is it important to read the notes if a company has commitments and contingencies?
    a. The notes contain the dollar amounts of those items that have not been disclosed in the balance sheet.
    b. The notes alert users to earnings management techniques.
    c. Commitments and contingencies are contractual agreements and potential liabilities that may impact the firm significantly in the future.
    d. None of the above
16. What accounts are most likely to be found in the shareholders' equity section of the statement of financial condition?
    a. Common stock, retained earnings, accumulated other comprehensive income
    b. Stock options, preferred stock, dividends payable
    c. Assets, liabilities, equity
    d. Common stock, properties, postemployment liabilities
17. What does the retained earnings account measure?
    a. Piles of unused cash
    b. The earnings distributed to shareholders
    c. The accumulation of all stock dividends and stock splits
    d. The sum of all the company's profits since it began operations, less any payments made to shareholders in the form of dividends
18. What is treasury stock?
    a. Stock sold by the U.S. Treasury
    b. Stock that has been repurchased by the company that originally issued it
    c. Stock that has been retired
    d. Stock that is issued in foreign markets

Chapter 4

Cash Flows—Operating, Financing, Investing

➤ Net income versus cash flow from operations

➤ Statement of cash flows

➤ How to read and interpret the statement of cash flows

➤ Focus on cash flow from operations

➤ CFO and three bankruptcies: Enron, Global Crossing®, and Kmart

➤ Caution flags for users of annual reports

➤ Test yourself

Something big is happening. Houses are talking to computers, magazines are talking to wireless phones, cars are talking to the Internet. It's already begun. We have entered the era in which things don't just think, but share what they know with one another. One company is at the heart of making it happen. Motorola.

—From front cover and inside pages Motorola 2000 Annual Report

Motorola *is* making it happen. In 2000, Motorola's earnings rose by $427 million—a whopping 48 percent increase over 1999—and basic earnings per share increased by 19 cents or 45 percent. This performance is especially impressive considering that Motorola had reported a net loss of $907 million as recently as 1998. The turnaround is to be commended, and Motorola does exactly that, commending itself through the first 20 pages of its 2000 annual report. The only minor glitch comes in the letter to stockholders, which briefly notes that the value of stockholders' investments in Motorola stock declined dramatically after reaching an all-time high early in the year.

It is not until page 24 of the annual report, which shows Motorola's consolidated statements of cash flows, that the reader finds any real clue to why investors responded as they did to Motorola's earnings reports in 2000, sending the stock price spiraling downward. The company generated no cash from its operations. In spite of the strong profit performance in 2000, Motorola had a negative cash flow from operating activities of more than $1 billion:

(in millions)	2000	1999	1998
Net earnings (loss)	$1,318	891	(907)
Net cash provided by (used for) operating activities	(1,164)	2,140	1,295

Source: Motorola, Inc. 2000 Annual Report.

In sharp contrast, Blockbuster Inc. is a company that had no earnings at all during the same period but managed to produce more than $1 billion in cash from operations during each of the 3 years:

(in millions)	2000	1999	1998
Net loss	$ (75.9)	(69.2)	(336.6)
Net cash flow provided by operating activities	1,320.8	1,142.8	1,234.5

Source: Blockbuster Inc. 2000 Annual Report.

How can one company, Motorola, report strong earnings but no cash, and another, Blockbuster, generate considerable amounts of cash from bottom line net losses? What about all the companies, such as Kodak, that fall somewhere in between these extremes? And so what? Why does cash flow from operations matter to investors, creditors, and employees? How is operating cash flow useful in analyzing a company's financial performance? What else from the statement of cash flows is important to readers of an annual report? These questions are explored in this chapter through an in-depth study of Kodak's statement of cash flows and the use of additional company examples.

Cash flow from operations is the amount of actual cash that a company has earned from its ongoing operations during the accounting period. Net income on the earnings statement, as explained in Chapter 2, is measured by accrual, not cash, accounting. Net income also includes items of revenue and expense that are unrelated to operations. Figuring out how much cash a company generates from day-to-day operations begins with net income on the earnings statement but adjusts that figure for items that have not actually produced or used cash, and which do not relate to operations.

In the case of Motorola, for instance, the company had large increases in both accounts receivable and inventory during 2000. Motorola's net income, figured on an accrual basis, included more sales revenue than was actually received in cash, and recognized less cost of goods sold expense than was actually paid for the purchase of inventory. When net income is adjusted to cash from operations, the increases in receivables and inventory are deducted. Among the other additional adjustments for Motorola were over $1.5 billion in gains on sales of investments and businesses during 2000. Because those gains are not part of operating income (the cash received is included in a firm's investing activities), they are deducted from net income in determining cash from operations. The combined result after all the adjustments was that Motorola actually produced no cash from its operating activities in 2000.

Blockbuster is the opposite case, beginning not with profit in 2000, but with a net loss of $75.9 million. One of the expense items in an earnings statement is depreciation. But depreciation is a "noncash" expense because, as explained in Chapter 2, it is the allocation of a cost previously made, not a current cash outlay. The same is true for amortization. When Blockbuster added back the $1,195 million deduction from income made for depreciation and amortization, it turns out the company actually generated cash from its operations during 2000. There are other adjustments for Blockbuster, but that is the primary one.

Readers might be interested to know how investors responded to the two companies' performance reports. Although cash flow from operations is not the only difference between Motorola and Blockbuster (see the discussion of both companies in Chapter 2), it is certainly a factor. The price movement of each firm's common stock indicates that investors made Blockbuster the clear winner:

Price per common share:	Motorola	Blockbuster
Year-end 2000	$20	8
Midyear 2001	17	18
Year-end 2001	15	26

Motorola's share price lost ground throughout 2001, while Blockbuster's rose significantly.

This chapter uses a two-step approach by (1) first explaining what is on a statement of cash flows and (2) discussing how to interpret the information presented, with an emphasis on cash flow from operations as an analytical tool in assessing financial performance.

The ongoing success of any business depends upon its ability to generate cash from its operations because it is cash that a firm needs to pay its employees and to satisfy investors and creditors. A positive net earnings figure is ultimately meaningless unless the company can translate profits into cash, and the only source of information about a company's ability to produce cash from operations is the statement of cash flows.

STATEMENT OF CASH FLOWS

The statement of cash flows provides information about cash inflows and outflows during an accounting period. Like the statements of earnings and shareholders' equity, this statement is presented for a 3-year period. On the statement, cash flows are separated by operating activities, investing activities, and financing activities.[1] The difference between all the cash inflows and all the cash outflows is the change in the cash (or cash and cash equivalents) account for the period.

---

[1] If a company has financing and investing activities that do not involve cash—such as the exchange of one piece of property for another—these activities are reported in a separate schedule.

Understanding the Corporate Annual Report

The "Consolidated Statement of Cash Flows for Eastman Kodak Company and Subsidiaries" is shown in Exhibit 4-1, with numbers added to the left of each item. Outflows of cash have parentheses, and inflows do not. To facilitate discussion of the statement, the explanation will focus on the year 2000.

Operating Activities

Operating activities are the first category reported on the statement of cash flows and involve the production and delivery of goods and services. Cash flows from operating activities are the cash effects of the transactions and events related to the firm's operations. On the statement of cash flows, the figure for cash flow from operating activities shows the amount of cash that has been generated internally, in contrast to financing and investing which are external activities. When a company is not able to generate sufficient cash internally, from operations, it turns to external sources. Motorola, for example, with its negative cash flow from operating activities, added more than $5 billion in new debt (a financing activity) during 2000.

The cash flow statement begins with the adjustments that are necessary to convert net income (prepared according to the accrual basis of accounting) to cash flow from operating activities. Companies have a choice of how to report these adjustments. Almost all companies, including Kodak, use the **indirect method** that begins with net income and adjusts for deferrals, accruals, noncash items, and nonoperating items. The **direct method** separately converts each item of revenue and expense from an earnings statement into a cash amount.

Kodak's statement of cash flows shows net earnings for the period of $1,407 million (line 1), and lines 2 through 9 are the items required to convert net income to cash (line 10) provided by operations—$982 million.[2]

1. Net earnings for the period were $1,407 million.
2. $889 million in depreciation and amortization expenses were added because they were noncash charges.
3. $117 million in gains on sales of businesses or assets were subtracted because the gain recognized did not generate operating cash; rather, the cash received from the sales was part of investing activities.
4. Restructuring costs, asset impairments, and other charges (none for 2000) were added back because they were noncash charges subtracted in calculating net earnings.
5. $235 million in deferred taxes was added because more expense was recognized on the earnings statement than was paid in cash for taxes.

---

[2] In accounting terminology, an inflow results from the decrease in an asset account, or an increase in a liability or equity account; an outflow results from the increase in an asset account or the decrease in a liability or equity account. Some of the adjustments cannot be reconciled to figures shown on the statement of financial condition because the company may have had write-offs of assets due to impairment, restructuring, or retirement; translation adjustments from foreign operations; acquisitions and dispositions of other companies; and simultaneous transactions not affecting cash.

To prepare the statement of cash flows, all the changes in balance sheet accounts are designated as inflows or outflows of cash and segregated by operating, investing, and financing activities. The inflows less the outflows balances to the change in cash or cash and cash equivalents account.

Exhibit 4-1

Eastman Kodak and Subsidiary Companies Consolidated Statement of Cash Flows

For the Year Ended December 31 (in millions)	2000	1999	1998
Cash flows from operating activities:			
1) Net earnings	$1,407	1,392	1,390
Adjustments to reconcile to net cash provided by operating activities:			
2) Depreciation and amortization	889	918	853
3) Gains on sales of businesses or assets	(117)	(162)	(166)
4) Restructuring costs, asset impairments, and other charges	—	453	42
5) Provision for deferred income taxes	235	247	202
6) Increase in receivables	(247)	(121)	(1)
7) Increase in inventories	(282)	(201)	(43)
8) Decrease in liabilities excluding borrowings	(755)	(478)	(516)
9) Other items, net	(148)	(115)	(278)
10) Net cash provided by operating activities	**982**	**1,933**	**1,483**
Cash flows from investment activities:			
11) Additions to properties	(945)	(1,127)	(1,108)
12) Proceeds from sales of businesses or assets	276	468	297
13) Cash flows related to sales of businesses	1	(46)	(59)
14) Acquisitions, net of cash acquired	(130)	(3)	(949)
15) Marketable securities—sales	84	127	162
16) Marketable securities—purchases	(69)	(104)	(182)
17) Net cash used in investment activities	**(783)**	**(685)**	**(1,839)**
Cash flows from financing activities:			
18) Net increase (decrease) in borrowings with original maturities of 90 days or less	939	(136)	894
19) Proceeds from other borrowings	1,310	1,343	1,133
20) Repayment of other borrowings	(936)	(1,118)	(1,251)
21) Dividends to shareholders	(545)	(563)	(569)
22) Exercise of employee stock options	43	44	128
23) Stock repurchase programs	(1,125)	(897)	(258)
24) Net cash (used in) provided by financing activities	**(314)**	**(1,327)**	**77**
25) Effect of exchange rate changes on cash	(12)	(5)	8
26) Net decrease in cash and cash equivalents	**(127)**	**(84)**	**(271)**
27) Cash and cash equivalents, beginning of year	373	457	728
28) Cash and cash equivalents, end of year	$ 246	373	457

6. The $247 million increase in receivables was subtracted because more sales revenue was recognized than was received in cash.

7. The $282 million increase in inventories was subtracted because less expense was recognized in cost of goods sold than was actually paid for inventories.

8. The $755 million decrease in liabilities excluding borrowings was subtracted because more cash was paid to suppliers and others than was recognized as an expense.

9. $148 million of other items were subtracted, reflecting changes in the "other" unspecified accrual and deferral accounts that affected net income.

Kodak produced cash from operations of $982 million (line 10), a positive amount but less than the $1,407 million (line 1) reported in net earnings as a result of these adjustments.

10. Cash from operations was $982 million.

Investing Activities

Investing activities include the acquisition or disposition of securities that are not cash equivalents; and productive assets, such as machinery and equipment, that are expected to benefit the firm for long periods of time. Investment activities also include lending money and collecting on loans.

Lines 11 through 16 show Kodak's investment activities.

11. $945 million was an outflow for the purchase of properties.
12. $276 million was an inflow from the sale of businesses and assets.
13. $1 million was an inflow related to the sales of business.
14. $130 million was an outflow for acquisitions.
15. $84 million was an inflow from selling marketable securities.
16. $69 million was an outflow from purchasing marketable securities.

Outflows exceeded inflows for Kodak's investment activities in 2000, resulting in net cash used in investment activities of $783 million (line 17).

17. $783 million net cash was used for investment activities.

Financing Activities

Financing activities include borrowing from creditors and repaying the principal; and obtaining resources from owners and providing owners with a return on investment. Kodak's cash inflows and outflows relating to financing activities are shown in lines 18 through 23, and net use of cash from financing activities in line 24.

18. $939 million was an inflow from short-term borrowings.
19. $1,310 million was an inflow from long-term borrowings.
20. $936 million was an outflow for repayments of long-term borrowings.
21. $545 million was an outflow for dividends paid to shareholders.
22. $43 million was an inflow from shares purchased by employees under stock option plans.
23. $1,125 million was an outflow for the repurchase of shares for employee programs.
24. Net use of cash from financing activities was $314 million in 2000.

Change in Cash

The bottom part of the statement shows the net change in Kodak's "cash and cash equivalents" account for 2000. Kodak had $373 million at the beginning of 2000 (line 27) and $246 million at year-end 2000 (line 28), resulting in the net decrease in cash and cash equivalents of $127 million (line 26).

The combination of operating, investing, and financing activities for Kodak and the effect of exchange rate changes produced this net decrease of $127 million in cash and cash equivalents (line 26). Looking separately at the categories for 2000, operations provided cash of $982 million (line 10); investing activities used cash of $783 million (line 17); financing activities used cash of $314 million (line 24); and there was a $12 million effect of exchange rate changes (line 25):

(in millions)	2000
Operating activities	$ 982
Investing activities	(783)
Financing activities	(314)
Exchange rate change	(12)
Change in cash and cash equivalents	$(127)

Kodak's operations provided cash, but its financing and investing activities used more cash than they have provided. There are no rules of thumb about what indicates successful cash management, but that is generally a desirable combination—with the day-to-day operations of the firm generating the cash that is used to invest in productive assets, repay debt, and pay dividends to shareholders.

What is troublesome for Kodak is the trend of cash flow from operations (downward) and its relationship to net earnings (less in 2000). That leads to the next step, which is to evaluate the information presented in a statement of cash flows and to consider its usefulness in assessing the company's condition and performance.

ANALYZING THE STATEMENT OF CASH FLOWS

Because the Financial Accounting Standards Board began requiring companies to prepare a statement of cash flows in the late 1980s, the information presented on this statement, and especially cash flow from operations, have become increasingly important in analyzing and valuing business firms. Ample evidence has been provided by companies in a range of sizes, shapes, and industries to document the fact that a firm can appear to be healthy when measured by net income but not be able to meet its obligations to creditors or pay dividends to shareholders; some even go bankrupt.

At the same time, it is important to emphasize that cash flow from operations alone is not a sufficient measure of how well a firm is doing, and any one single period's report cannot offer a complete picture of a firm's financial health. New, growing companies frequently do not generate any cash from operations in the early years of operations whereas established companies may be producing cash but still not be performing well.

In evaluating the material presented on a statement of cash flows it is useful to consider the trend and fluctuation of cash flow from operations over time as well as its relationship to net income. Generally, net income and cash flow from operations should track closely together.[3] If they don't, something may be out of whack. For example, if net income is rising but cash flow from operations is declining, this may be a signal that the company has uncollectable accounts receivables or unsalable inventory; it may be the company is playing games with its accounting methods or recognizing sizable amounts of nonoperating income, such as selling off assets. But negative cash from operations can also mean that the company is actually growing in a healthy way and is temporarily using operating cash to do that.

Always, it is necessary to consider the underlying causes of trends that appear to be out of line in some way and to look at a company's performance for more than one accounting period. It is also important for readers to be aware that cash flow from operations can be manipulated. For example, a company can choose not to pay off accounts payable at the end of an accounting period, which would temporarily improve cash flow from operations.

Other sections of the statement of cash flows provide useful information about the company's cash needs from external sources, its ability to meet fixed obligations, how well it is managing productive assets and investments, and its ability to satisfy owners through dividend payments and healthy growth. If the company is not generating cash from operations, the statement is revealing in showing what external sources are being used to provide needed cash.

Free Cash Flow

In addition to cash flow from operations, a widely used analytical tool is **free cash flow,** which considers the need for companies to provide cash not only for current operations but to expand with new capital investment. There is, unfortunately, no standardized accounting measure for free cash flow. Some commonly used measures of free cash flow begin with cash flow from operating activities and deduct capital expenditures or both capital expenditures and dividend payments to shareholders, which would be the cash left over to grow beyond existing commitments. Some analysts adjust earnings before interest, taxes, depreciation, and amortization (EBITDA) for changes in working capital, income taxes, capital expenditures, and nonrecurring items such as gains or losses from the sale of assets. When reference is made to free cash flow, the reader should look behind the number to determine how it is calculated.

Blockbuster's earnings reports, not surprisingly, feature free cash flow rather than the firm's net losses calculated by accrual accounting. Blockbuster measures free cash flow as net income before depreciation and amortization less capital expenditures.

Kodak's statement of cash flows is used in this section to illustrate how to read and interpret a statement of cash flows, but we hope that this same approach is useful to readers of any company's cash flow statement. Exhibit 4-2 presents a summary to facilitate the analysis of a statement of cash flows by separating the statement into inflows and outflows for the 3-year period. That allows readers to see exactly what areas are contributing cash (inflows) and what areas are using cash (outflows). Inflows are shown on the top of the statement in both dollar amounts and as a percentage of total inflows; and outflows are shown on the bottom half, in dollar amounts and as a percentage of total outflows.

---

[3] An interesting article on this topic is "Mind the Gap," *CFO*, November 2000, which includes a quantitative measurement of the gap between growth in earnings and growth in cash flow from operations.

Exhibit 4-2

Eastman Kodak Company Summary Analysis Statement of Cash Flows

	2000	%	1999	%	1998	%
Inflows (in millions)						
Operating activities	$ 982	27.0	1,933	49.4	1,483	36.1
Proceeds from sales of businesses/assets	276	7.6	468	12.0	297	7.2
Cash flows related to sales of businesses	1	0.0	0	0.0	0	0.0
Marketable securities—sales	84	2.3	127	3.2	162	4.0
Net increase in borrowings (90 days or less)	939	25.9	0	0.0	894	21.8
Proceeds from other borrowings	1,310	36.0	1,343	34.3	1,133	27.6
Exercise of employee stock options	43	1.2	44	1.1	128	3.1
Effect of exchange rate changes on cash	0	0.0	0	0.0	8	0.2
Total Inflows	$3,635	100.0	3,915	100.0	4,105	100.0
Outflows (in millions)						
Additions to properties	$ 945	25.1	1,127	28.2	1,108	25.3
Cash flows related to sales of businesses	0	0.0	46	1.1	59	1.3
Acquisitions, net of cash acquired	130	3.5	3	0.1	949	21.7
Marketable securities—purchases	69	1.8	104	2.6	182	4.2
Decrease in borrowings (90 days or less)	0	0.0	136	3.4	0	0.0
Repayments of other borrowings	936	24.9	1,118	28.0	1,251	28.6
Dividends to shareholders	545	14.5	563	14.1	569	13.0
Stock repurchase programs	1,125	29.9	897	22.4	258	5.9
Effect of exchange rate changes on cash	12	0.3	5	0.1	0	0.0
Total Outflows	$3,762	100.0	3,999	100.0	4,376	100.0
Net decrease in cash and cash equivalents	(127)		(84)		(271)	

In his 2000 Letter to Shareholders, the Kodak Chairman says

> It might be wise to seek companies that are adept at generating cash. Those are the firms that will continue to invest in themselves and prepare for growth, regardless of the economy. And that, as you might have already surmised, brings us to Kodak.

Let's see if the information on the statement of cash flows confirms the chairman's evaluation of Kodak's adeptness in generating cash, investing in itself, and preparing for growth.

Inflows

The first category in Exhibit 4–2 is operating activities, and the figures show that Kodak *was* producing cash from operations in all 3 years, but the amounts fluctuated considerably, and the overall trend was declining. Kodak provided almost 50 percent of its cash internally in 1999 but only 27 percent in 2000.

What external sources of cash did Kodak use when cash flow from operations fell so sharply? The exhibit shows the answer quite clearly. Borrowings provided 61.9 percent (25.9 percent borrowings with maturities of 90-days or less and 36.0 percent from other borrowings) of Kodak's cash in 2000, compared with 34.3 percent in 1999. The other major source of cash was selling off businesses and assets, which could not exactly be described as investing in itself.

Outflows

How did Kodak use its cash? Additions to properties does potentially indicate growth, and Kodak used 25 percent to 28 percent of its cash for new properties over the 3-year period. About the same amount, however, was needed for debt service, and that will rise in the future as a result of the increased borrowings in 2000. Note also that Kodak used over $900 million (21.7 percent of total outflows) for acquisitions in 1998, but only $130 million (3.5 percent of total outflows) in 2000.

Further adding to the need for borrowed funds are the stock repurchase programs initiated in 1996, 1999, and 2000. As discussed in Chapter 2, repurchases have the effect of increasing earnings per share because fewer shares are outstanding. The Board of Directors of Kodak authorized a total of $6 billion to be used to acquire treasury stock. In 1999 and 2000, 22.4 percent and 29.9 percent, respectively, of total cash outflows were used to repurchase stock. On average Kodak repurchased stock for $75 per share under the 1996 program and $56 per share under the 1999 program.

In the management's discussion and analysis (MD&A) section of the 1999 annual report, the stock repurchase program strategy was explained. Management stated that the company plans "to repurchase shares at a level at least sufficient to eliminate year-on-year dilution from the exercise of the company-sponsored employee stock option program as well as management incentive option grants." A relatively small portion of stock repurchased has in fact been used for employee stock plans. Over the past 3 years Kodak has repurchased 38,600,662 shares and issued 6,016,805 shares under employee plans. Given Kodak's declining stock price, it is unlikely that the company will realize gains should they resell this stock on the open market. One has to question the use of borrowed funds for stock repurchases when cash flow from operations does not cover capital expenditures, debt payments, and dividends.

Response to Kodak's Chairman

The following exhibit shows Kodak's tumbling stock price for the 4 quarters of the year following the chairman's statement:

KODAK COMMON STOCK

Price per Share, 2001	High	Low
First Quarter	$46.65	38.19
Second Quarter	49.95	37.76
Third Quarter	47.38	30.75
Fourth Quarter	36.10	24.40

Investors seemed to agree with Kodak's chairman that it would be wise to seek companies that are generating cash, investing in themselves, and preparing for growth—which apparently *did not* bring them to Kodak during 2001.

FOCUS ON CASH FLOW FROM OPERATIONS

The discussion of Kodak's statement of cash flows has so far considered what the statement of cash flows shows, how to interpret that information, and the possible impact of cash flows on the perceptions of investors in valuing a company. In analyzing the statement of cash flows, it is important to evaluate not only a firm's success in generating cash internally over time, but the underlying causes for the trends and fluctuations of a firm's cash flow from operations.

Exhibit 4-3 shows the portion of Kodak's statement of cash flows that lists the adjustments made to net earnings (1) to calculate cash flow from operating activities. Earlier in the chapter, each of these adjustments was explained. The intent now is to determine what information they provide about the company that is useful to readers of an annual report.

For almost all companies, the first add-back is depreciation or depreciation and amortization (2). This amount relates to a company's investments in long-lived assets. The fact that the amount of Kodak's depreciation and amortization expense decreased in 2000 reflects the shrinking asset base that was noted in Chapter 3. Even though there were new capital expenditures in 2000, the overall investment in capital assets was reduced. Kodak's statement of financial condition shows that "land, buildings, and equipment" and "goodwill" declined between 1999 and 2000:

At December 31 (in millions)	2000	1999
Land, buildings, and equipment at cost	$12,963	13,289
Goodwill (net of accumulated amortization)	947	982

Source: Eastman Kodak Annual Report 2000.

The adjustments also comprised eliminating the effect of any items that were included in net income but did not generate operating cash—taking out the gains on sales of businesses and assets (3) because all of the cash from these sales was included in investing activities.

Restructuring charges and asset impairments (4) were added back because they were noncash charges that were subtracted in calculating net income.

The deferred taxes adjustments (5) were the result of using different accounting methods for reporting and tax purposes. Overall, Kodak paid less in taxes than was reported on the earnings statement, and this is a common situation, especially for companies with relatively heavy investments in capital assets. Even though Kodak's long-lived assets declined, they still constitute more than 40 percent of Kodak's total assets.

The effect of the changes in working capital (current assets and current liabilities) accounts are extremely important to most companies' success in generating cash flow from operating activities, and that is certainly the case for Kodak. Note that in

Exhibit 4-3

Eastman Kodak and Subsidiary Companies Cash Flows from Operating Activities

FOR THE YEAR ENDED DECEMBER 31, (IN MILLIONS)	2000	1999	1998
Cash flows from operating activities:			
1) Net earnings	$1,407	1,392	1,390
Adjustments to reconcile to net cash provided by operating activities:			
2) Depreciation and amortization	889	918	853
3) Gains on sales of businesses and assets	(117)	(162)	(166)
4) Restructuring costs, asset impairments, and other charges	—	453	42
5) Provision for deferred income taxes	235	247	202
6) Increase in receivables	(247)	(121)	(1)
7) Increase in inventories	(282)	(201)	(43)
8) Decrease in liabilities excluding borrowings	(755)	(478)	(516)
9) Other items, net	(148)	(115)	(278)
10) Net cash provided by operating activities	982	1,933	1,483

all 3 years the impact of the changes in Kodak's receivables, inventories, and liabilities (6, 7, and 8) other than borrowings was a deduction from net income. For a start-up company, rapid growth in inventories and accounts receivables might be expected, but that was not the case for Kodak. The fact that inventories and receivables were increasing but sales were relatively flat was not a positive development, and the cash flow statement underscores the effect on cash. The reduction in liabilities meant that Kodak was, on a net basis, paying out more in cash to suppliers and for other liabilities than was recorded as an expense on the earnings statement—in other words, Kodak was getting less credit from its suppliers, even though inventory was rising. Some of the "other liabilities" number was also affected by Kodak's restructuring programs.

Finally, it is important to look at the relationship between net earnings (1) and cash flow from operating activities over time (10):

Kodak (in millions)	2000	1999	1998
Cash provided by operating activities	$ 982	1,933	1,482
Net earnings	1,407	1,392	1,390
Difference	$ (425)	541	92

In the 3-year period for Kodak, cash flow from operating activities was positive in all 3 years, but was much lower than net earnings in 2000, much higher in 1999, and slightly higher in 1998. Net earnings and cash flow from operating activities did not track closely for Kodak, underscoring some of the company's apparent weaknesses. Note also that the main cause of the "bulge" in 1999 was the timing of the restructuring charges, discussed in Chapter 2 as Kodak's "big bath."

Although the adjustments to net earnings shown in Kodak's statement of cash flows are specific to Kodak, the general categories are similar among most companies. They involve the working capital accounts such as accounts receivable, inventories, and accounts payable that are affected by accrual accounting, depreciation and amortization expense, deferred income taxes, and items that have been included in net income but are not part of a company's ongoing, day-to-day operations.

BIG BANKRUPTCIES

Given the importance of cash flow from operations in assessing a company's financial health, one would expect to find some hint of trouble revealed by a company's cash flow from operations prior to bankruptcy. A review of the cash flow statements for Enron, Global Crossing, and Kmart confirm the expectations, but not from the amount of operating cash flow reported. In the year before declaring bankruptcy, all three companies recorded strong, positive cash flow from operating activities.

Enron filed for bankruptcy in December 2001. For the year ended December 31, 2000, Enron reported $979 million in net income and cash flow from operating activities of more than $4.8 billion. One of the elements discussed earlier in the chapter to consider in analyzing cash flow is the relationship between net income and cash flow from operations—the two should generally track fairly closely together. The following exhibit shows Enron's reported net income compared with cash flow from operations for the period 1998–2000:

Enron Corporation (in millions)	2000	1999	1998
Net income	$ 979	893	703
Net cash provided by operating activities	4,779	1,228	1,640

Although the growth of net income was smooth and upward, the trend of cash flow from operating activities was not. Cash flow from operations was positive, but the fluctuations were enormous, and the 2000 gain was widely out of line with the growth in net income. The Chapter 1 discussion of Enron revealed the same erratic pattern for earlier years and raised one of the first caution flags in the book.

Determining why cash flow was so much higher ($3,800 million) than net income for Enron in 2000 requires a review of the adjustments to net income that were discussed in the previous section for Kodak. Unfortunately, the bulk of the difference was not explained, either in the notes or on the statement. The two biggest adjustments involved additions to net income for "other operating activities" of $1,113 million, which were not defined, and "changes in components of working capital" of $1,769 million which were listed:

Receivables (in millions)	$(8,203)
Inventories	1,336
Payables	7,167
Other	1,469
Total	$ 1,769

That breakdown shows that the huge increase (increase is shown in parentheses because it is deducted) in Enron's receivables of $8,203 million was more than offset by a $1,336 million reduction in inventory, a $7,167 million increase in payables,[4] and who knows what was in the other $1,469 million. Of the total $3,800 million difference between net income and cash flow from operations, $1,113 was unexplained "other operating activities," and $1,469 was unexplained "other " working capital; further, the changes in receivables, inventories, and payables were not discussed. What management did say about operating cash flow was the following: "Net cash provided by operating activities increased $3,551 million in 2000, primarily reflecting decreases in working capital, positive operating results and a receipt of cash associated with the assumption of a contractual obligation." At least Enron was consistent in its obtuseness.

Global Crossing, Ltd. is the telecommunications firm that filed for bankruptcy in January 2002. In its third quarter report, which included results for 9 months of 2001, the company had a loss of $4.6 billion but positive cash flow from operations of $418 million. The reasons for the positive cash flow from operations were adjustments to the reported net loss that took out nonoperating items—losses on the sales of businesses and over $2 billion on the write-down of investments. Investing activities were also positive for Global Crossing because of cash generated from selling a business (that was sold at a loss). Global Crossing's financing activities provided cash because the company added over $4 billion in new long-term debt in 2001.

The retailer Kmart also filed for bankruptcy in January 2002. For its fiscal year ending January 31, 2001, Kmart reported a net loss of $244 million but positive cash flows from operating activities of more than $1,039 million. To account for this difference Kmart's cash flow statement revealed that two of the biggest adjustments to net income were a "one-time charge for strategic actions" and a "decrease in inventories." Deep in the notes, it turned out that the "one-time charge for strategic actions" meant store closings, and that was also the reason for the sharp decline in inventories.

These three company examples illustrate the importance of considering not just a firm's success or failure in generating cash from operations, but also the underlying causes of the positive or negative cash flow, the relationship between operating cash flow and net income, and fluctuations in cash flow from operations over time. It is also important to remember that cash flow from operations is one of many essential pieces that are useful in analyzing a company's financial condition and performance.

READERS' CHECKLIST OF CAUTION FLAGS FROM CHAPTER 4

➤ Failure to generate cash from operating activities
➤ Large fluctuations in cash flow from operating activities over time
➤ Net income and cash flow from operations not tracking closely

➤ Net income and cash flow from operations moving in different directions
➤ Positive cash flow from investing activities because company is selling off assets to generate cash

---

[4] To adjust net income to cash flow from operations, increases in current assets and decreases in current liabilities are subtracted; decreases in current assets and increases in current liabilities are added.

➢ Positive cash flow from financing activities for several periods—possibly indicating borrowing needed to offset lack of internal cash generation
➢ Company highlights cash flow in shareholders' letter, especially in same paragraph discussing falling stock price

➢ Adjustments to net income from changes in receivables, inventories, and payables not in line with sales
➢ Management's explanations of adjustments to net income obtuse or missing

TEST YOURSELF

Solutions are provided immediately following the Glossary at the end of the book.

1. What information is presented on a statement of cash flows?
   a. The cash inflows and cash outflows during an accounting period
   b. Cash flow from operating, investing, and financing activities
   c. Information to explain the change in the cash account for the period
   d. All of the above

2. Which of the following statements is false?
   a. Cash generated from operating activities is internally generated cash, whereas cash generated from investing or financing activities is externally generated cash.
   b. Investing activities include borrowings and repayments of borrowings.
   c. Financing activities include items related to borrowings and items related to common stock.
   d. Depreciation and amortization are added back to net income in calculating cash flow from operating activities.

3. Why are cash flows from operating activities and net income not the same?
   a. Net income excludes operating income.
   b. Net income is measured by accrual, not cash, accounting.
   c. Net income is measured by cash, not accrual, accounting.
   d. Cash flows from operating activities are measured by accrual accounting.

4. If cash flows from operating activities are positive, but cash flows from financing and investing activities are negative, the cash account would:
   a. Increase
   b. Decrease
   c. Remain the same
   d. Cannot be determined without knowing amounts of positive and negative cash flows

5. Which of the following cash flows would management most want to be positive each year?
   a. Operating
   b. Investing
   c. Financing
   d. Exchange rate change

6. If cash flow from operating activities is declining, what might this indicate?
   a. The company has uncollectable accounts receivable or unsalable inventory.
   b. The company is expanding operations and is temporarily using operating cash.

c. Both (a) and (b)

d. None of the above

7. Which of the following items would be sources of cash for a firm?

a. Borrowings, issuance of common stock, cash collections from sales

b. Repurchase of stock, borrowings, repayment of borrowings

c. Additions to properties, cash from operations, selling off assets

d. Acquisitions, borrowings, payments of cash dividends

8. Which of the following items would be uses of cash for a firm?

a. Sales of marketable securities, borrowings, cash payments for inventory

b. Acquisitions, borrowings, issuance of common stock

c. Sale of a business, cash from operations, repayment of borrowings

d. Acquisitions, repayment of borrowings, payment of cash dividends

9. What can be learned by analyzing a company's cash flow from operations?

a. Cash flow from operations highlights the relationship between net earnings and cash flow from operations.

b. The effect of changes in working capital accounts can offer insight into why cash flow from operations and net earnings differ.

c. Possible weaknesses in the company can be identified when net earnings and cash flow from operations do not track closely.

d. All of the above

10. Which of the following is not a caution flag for the statement of cash flows?

a. Failure to generate cash from operating activities

b. Net income and cash flow from operations moving in different directions

c. Positive cash flow from investing activities that indicates firm is borrowing

d. Adjustments to net income from changes in receivables, inventories, and payables not in line with sales

11. Which number from the financial statements should users focus on when determining how well a firm is performing?

a. Net earnings

b. Cash flow from operations

c. EBITDA adjusted for changes in working capital

d. No one number can offer a complete picture of how a firm is performing.

12. Which of the following statements is true about the bankruptcies of Enron, Global Crossing, and Kmart?

a. All three companies recorded negative cash from operations prior to their bankruptcy filings.

b. All three companies recorded positive cash from operations prior to their bankruptcy filings.

c. All three companies had net earnings numbers that were almost identical to their cash from operations numbers.

d. All three companies were closing stores, but did not reveal this in their notes.

Chapter 5

A Comprehensive Analysis

➤ *Objectives of analysis*
➤ *Sources of information*
➤ *Tools and techniques*
➤ *Comprehensive analysis of Kodak*
➤ *Caution flags for users of annual reports*
➤ *Test yourself*

The previous chapters have covered in detail the individual pieces of a corporate annual report, including some analysis, as each financial statement was presented and discussed. This chapter broadens the framework to illustrate a comprehensive analysis that integrates all of the financial statements with other information in an annual report, and some additional resources outside of the report. The objective is to provide an *approach* to analysis that offers a wide variety of analytical techniques from which readers can choose what to use in addressing specific objectives.

One of the helpful elements used in interpreting financial statement data, for example, is a set of financial ratios. Financial ratios incorporate numbers from all of the financial statements in various combinations to focus on specific areas of a company's financial condition and performance. From the detailed list of ratios defined and discussed in this chapter, users can select what they need for a particular purpose, such as making a decision about investing in securities or whether to lend money to a firm or if the company should make new capital expenditures. The intent is to equip readers with the tools of analysis that are useful in interpreting the material presented in any set of corporate financial statements,[1] regardless of the users' individual perspective.

OBJECTIVES OF ANALYSIS

The first step in evaluating a firm's financial reports is to specify the **objectives of the analysis.** The questions addressed vary somewhat depending upon a user's individual area of interest.

An **investor** uses the historical record of a company to arrive at an estimate of its future potential and value. In deciding whether to buy, hold, or sell a firm's securities, the investment analysis includes consideration of such questions as:

What is the company's record with regard to growth and stability of earnings? Of cash flow from operations? Is management hyping one or more performance measures and, if so, why?

How much risk is inherent in the firm's financial structure? What are the expected returns, given the company's current condition and future outlook? Is the company's management attempting to hide or obscure any important information related to risk?

How does the firm's operating performance compare with its industry competitors? How well positioned is the company to hold or improve its competitive position? What is its strategy with regard to capital expenditures and discretionary expenses such as research and development?

A **creditor** ultimately needs to assess the company's ability to meet cash needs as they arise, in particular the interest and principal payments on borrowed funds. A credit analyst would raise such questions as:

Why is the company borrowing? What do the financial statements reveal about borrowing cause? Is the firm generating cash from operations? Does the firm need funds to support healthy operations and growth or to cover inadequate cash production?

What is the firm's existing capital structure and proportion of debt? How well does the firm service its existing debt?

What will be the source of debt repayment? How effectively does the company manage working capital? How has the firm provided and used cash in the past—from operating, financing, and investing activities?

The management of a firm not only prepares the financial reports but also relies on the information presented. Company management and boards of directors need to address all of the above questions that are relevant to investors and creditors, as

---

[1]Except specialized industries, such as banking, real estate, and public utilities; even for those industries, much of the material in the chapter is relevant to analysis.

well as those raised by employees, competitors, and suppliers, because all of these user groups must be satisfied in order for the firm to continue to operate and prosper. Management must also consider responses to its financial reporting by the general public, regulators, and the financial press. Managers and directors want to determine answers to questions such as:

How well has the company performed and why? What operating areas have contributed to success and which have not?

What are the firm's strengths and weaknesses? How are areas of strength and weakness affecting the company's actual financial condition and performance as well as external perceptions of the company?

How successfully have the company's strategies and policies been implemented? What changes should be made to improve future operations?

Financial reporting occurs in an environment that is potentially adversarial. A company's management wants to present the most positive picture possible in the firm's financial reports, whereas readers of the information want a picture that most clearly reflects financial reality. Using corporate annual reports for business decision-making—regardless of the reader's perspective or purpose—requires an informed interpretation of the picture presented in the financial statements. The approach taken in this book is to provide readers with a broad overview of analysis rather than to focus on the specific questions of any one user group. We hope that this comprehensive approach to interpreting financial reports supplies the tools and techniques needed for meeting a wide range of reader objectives.

SOURCES OF INFORMATION

Financial Statements and Notes

The primary resource for evaluating a firm's financial condition and performance is the set of four financial statements covered in Chapters 2, 3, and 4: the earnings or income statement; the statement of financial condition or balance sheet; the statement of shareholders' equity; and the statement of cash flows. Management has the responsibility for preparing the financial statements, and as has been discussed, management also has the potential to influence the outcome of financial statement reporting in order to appeal to investors, creditors, employees, and other users. It is essential that the analysis of a company's financial statements include a careful reading of relevant notes to the financial statements and to supplement the review with other material in an annual report and possibly information separate from the report.

The objective of the analysis determines to a considerable extent not only the approach taken but the sources of information that will be relevant to a particular circumstance and the analytical techniques employed. The starting point, however, should always be the financial statements. In addition, the reader may want to consult some or all of the following resources.

Form 10-K and Form 10-Q

Form 10-K (discussed in Chapter 1) is an annual document filed with the SEC by companies that sell securities to the public and contains much of the same information as the annual report issued to shareholders. The 10-K report, however, contains additional detail that may be relevant to an analysis—including schedules showing information about management, a description of material litigation and governmental actions, and elaborations of some financial statement disclosures. The 10-Q reports provide quarterly financial statements (unaudited) and supplementary information. These documents are available to the public and for most companies can be accessed on the Web at www.edgar-online.com or on individual company Web sites.

Proxy Statement

The SEC requires publicly held companies to issue a proxy statement to shareholders prior to shareholder meetings. This document contains potentially useful material not available in the annual report. The proxy statement includes such information as biographical material about nominated directors, the firm's proposed auditing firm, amounts paid for audit and nonaudit services, oversight committees (such as audit and compensation), the number of shares held by the firm's owners and management, executive compensation packages, director compensation, proposed changes in compensation plans, and company relationships and related party transactions.

Auditors' Report

The report of the independent auditor expresses an opinion about the fairness of a company's financial statement presentation. Most auditors' reports are unqualified, which means that in the opinion of the auditor, the financial statements fairly present the firm's financial position, results of operations, and cash flows for the periods covered. A qualified report, adverse opinion, or disclaimer of opinion is rare but suggests serious problems. An unqualified opinion with explanatory language, which is more common, should be reviewed for the cause of the explanation. The content of auditors' reports and issues involving problems in reliance on auditors' reports were discussed in Chapter 1.

Management Discussion and Analysis

The "Management Discussion and Analysis" section (also discussed in Chapter 1 and cited in Chapters 2–4) is required and monitored by the SEC. In this section, management presents detailed coverage of the firm's liquidity, capital resources, and operations. This information can be especially helpful because it contains facts, estimates, explanations, and forward-looking information not presented in the financial statement or notes to the financial statements. Management must disclose any favorable or unfavorable trends and significant events or uncertainties that relate to the firm's historical or prospective financial condition and operations.

Supplementary Schedules

Firms like Kodak, that operate in several unrelated lines of business and that have operations outside of the United States, are required to include in the annual report certain supplementary schedules related to these operations, showing key financial information. The material provided in these segmental and geographic schedules is integrated into the comprehensive analysis of Kodak.

Other Sources

There is a considerable body of material outside of the corporate annual report that can be useful in the evaluation of a company's financial statements. Most academic libraries and many public libraries have available computerized search systems and computerized databases that can greatly facilitate financial analysis.[2] Although not a replacement for the techniques that are discussed in this chapter, these research materials supplement and enhance the analytical process and provide time-saving features.

Comparative statistical ratios can be useful in the analysis of financial statements by showing how well the company operates relative to its competitors. Some or all of the following sources may be accessed in public libraries:

1. Dun and Bradstreet Information Services, *Industry Norms and Key Business Ratios.* Murray Hill, NJ
2. Robert Morris Associates, *Annual Statement Studies.* Philadelphia, PA
3. Standard & Poor's Corporation, *Ratings Handbook and Industry Surveys.* New York, NY
4. Gale Research Inc., *Manufacturing U.S.A. Industry Analyses.* Detroit, MI

The resource used to compare Kodak to its competitors is the Robert Morris Associates (RMA) publication, *Annual Statement Studies.*The publication contains calculations of industry averages by industry using the standard industrial classification (SIC) number. The SIC number for a company can be found on the front page of the Form 10-K report (on the SEC EDGAR database). Kodak's SIC number is 3861 and the industry is "Manufacturing-Photographic Equipment and Supplies."

Detailed data are generally available from RMA to compare companies of like sizes, but for Kodak, RMA only offers detailed information for companies having $10 to $25 million of sales. Because Kodak is much larger, the industry average used in this book is a general average of all companies found under the heading "Comparative Historical Data" 4/1/99–3/31/00. Thirty-eight companies are included in this average, but the names of the companies are not revealed. When consulting any publication such as RMA, it is important to read the legend and information on how to use the publication, usually located in the front of the book. Comparisons can also be made by using comparable ratios for a specific competitor or groups of competitors. It would be appropriate to compare Kodak's ratios, for example, with ratios for Canon, Fuji Films, and Sony.

---

[2] One resource that is commonly available in both public and academic libraries is the Infotrak—General Business Index. This CD-ROM database provides indexing to approximately 800 business, trade, and management journals; it has company profiles, investment analyst reports, and a wide range of business news. To learn about the availability and use of this system or other search systems and databases, consult the library's reference librarian or the business reference librarian.

Additional resources for comparative and other information about companies can be found on the following free Internet sites:[3]

1. Yahoo
2. Multex Investor

Many other Internet sites charge subscription fees to access information, but public and university libraries often subscribe, making this information free to the public. Libraries are currently in the process of converting information from hard-copy format to online databases; the following useful references may be available at a local library:

1. Moody's Investor Service, *Mergent Manuals and Mergent Handbook.* New York, NY (formerly Moody's Manuals and Handbook—online version is *Mergent FIS Online and Mergent Industry Surveys Disc*)
2. Standard & Poor's Corporation, *Corporation Records, The Outlook, Stock Reports, and Stock Guide.* New York, NY (online version is *Standard & Poor's Net Advantage*)
3. Value Line, Inc., *The Value Line Investment Survey.* New York, NY
4. Zack's Investment Research Inc., *Earnings Forecaster.* Chicago, IL
5. Gale Research Inc., *Market Share Reporter.* Detroit, MI
6. Dow Jones-Irwin, *The Financial Analyst's Handbook.* Homewood, IL
7. For mutual funds: Morningstar, *Morningstar Mutual Funds.* Chicago, IL

The following Web sites contain useful investment and financial information including company profile and stock price; some sites charge fees for certain information:

1. SEC EDGAR Database <www.sec.gov/edgarhp.htm>
2. Hoover's Corporate Directory
3. Dun & Bradstreet
4. Standard & Poor's Ratings Services
5. CNN Financial Network

Articles from current periodicals such as *Business Week, Forbes, Fortune,* and *The Wall Street Journal* can add insight into the management and operations of individual firms and provide perspective on general economic and industry trends. Many articles from relevant publications are cited in footnotes throughout this book.

There are also computerized financial statement analysis spreadsheet packages, such as Microsoft® Excel, that can be helpful in the analytical process. With this software, users can develop a template of the financial ratios—as defined in this chapter or from some other source—and then plug in numbers from the financial statements, with the program performing calculation of the ratios. The template can be set up in a way that allows comparisons of ratios across multiple years' financial data. Even with such number-crunching shortcuts, however, it is essential to understand what the financial ratios measure and are intended to show. (Translated, that means you still have to read the rest of the chapter.)

---

[3] Internet sites are constantly changing; therefore, the content and Web addresses may change after publication of this book.

TOOLS AND TECHNIQUES

There are a variety of tools and techniques that help convert financial statement presentations into formats that facilitate analysis. These include

- common size financial statements discussed in Chapter 2 (common size income statement) and Chapter 3 (common size balance sheet);
- the summary analysis statement of cash flows shown in Chapter 4;
- financial ratios, which standardize financial statement data in terms of mathematical relationships expressed in the form of percentages or times;
- trend analysis, which evaluates financial data over several accounting periods;
- structural analysis, which considers the internal composition of a firm;
- industry comparisons, which relate one firm with averages compiled for the industry in which it operates; and
- the most important tool of all, a reader's common sense and judgment.

The tools and techniques of financial statement analysis will be explained and demonstrated through an analysis of Kodak, beginning with a review of the environment and economy in which the firm operates.

Background: Firm, Industry, and Economy

Firm

Eastman Kodak Company is the world's largest manufacturer of photographic film.[4] The company operates in four distinct segments: Consumer Imaging, Kodak Professional, Health Imaging, and Other Imaging. The Consumer Imaging and Kodak Professional segments obtain revenues from sales of film, paper, chemicals, cameras, photo processing equipment, digitization services, and other services to consumers and professional customers. The Health Imaging segment services the healthcare industry through sales of medical film and processing equipment. The Other Imaging segment sells motion picture film to the entertainment industry and microfilm equipment, document imaging software, consumer digital cameras, and media to commercial and government customers. Kodak manufactures and sells its products globally.[5]

Unexpected changes in Kodak management occurred in 2000. Former President and 29-year veteran of Kodak, Daniel A. Carp, took over the CEO position on January 1, 2000, replacing George Fisher (whose contract did not expire until December 31, 2000). Fisher, former chairman of Motorola, had been brought in as CEO in 1993 to move Kodak into the digital age. Although Fisher has moved Kodak into the digital world, he left the CEO position before the job was finished. Daniel Carp's expertise lies in brand-building, not high technology—the question is whether Carp can build the same type of brand recognition in technology as Kodak has in the film market. Kodak has a reputation as a "stodgy" company, not as an innovative firm that embraces change, and it is unknown whether the naming of Carp as CEO will move Kodak forward or backward.[6]

---

4 Hoover's Online, Eastman Kodak Company, Company Capsule (March 1, 2002).
5 Eastman Kodak Company Annual Report (2000), pp. 61, 63.
6 William Symonds, Geoffrey Smith, and Paul Judge, "Fisher's Photofinish," *Business Week* (June 21, 1999), p. 34.

Industry

Kodak faces fierce competition in all markets. Even though Kodak is still the market leader in film, its main competitor, Fuji Photo Film, has rapidly been closing the gap. Price wars in the film market have negatively affected Kodak, which derives over half its revenues from film. In the digital market, the competition is even stiffer. Kodak's two key competitors are Sony and Canon. Kodak ranked second behind Sony for digital camera sales in August 1999. Its 17 percent share was far behind Sony's 52 percent share; Kodak has not yet turned a profit on digital cameras. The lack of profitability, combined with intense competition and the fact that a digital camera customer is no longer a film-purchasing customer, yields a bleak picture for Kodak in the digital industry.[7] One bright spot in Kodak's strategy has been the installation of some 19,000 highly profitable Picture Maker Kiosks at retail stores. These kiosks allow customers to edit and print images from negatives, CDs, or digital camera memory cards. Most kiosk customers are repeat customers, thereby adding to photo paper sales.[8]

Economy

The current economic outlook is not especially promising. The year 2000 brought an overall economic slowdown, the dot-com bubble burst, and technology firms have been hit hard by both events. Kodak is experiencing a deterioration of its core film sales as consumers and professionals switch to more innovative digital products. The current economic downturn couldn't have come at a worse time for Kodak, as it tries to transition from a mature, stable market that is now disappearing, to the high-growth technology sector.

Key Financial Ratios

Numbers from Kodak's financial statements are used to illustrate how to calculate and interpret a set of key financial ratios, divided into four broad categories: (1) liquidity ratios, which measure the firm's ability to meet cash needs as they arise; (2) activity ratios, which measure the liquidity of specific assets and the firm's efficiency in managing assets; (3) leverage ratios, which measure the extent of a firm's financing with debt relative to equity (capital structure), and its ability to cover interest and other fixed charges; and (4) profitability ratios, which measure the overall performance of a firm and its efficiency in managing assets, liabilities, and equity.

Some words of caution are important regarding the use of financial ratios. Although extremely valuable as analytical tools, financial ratios also have limitations. These ratios can serve as screening devices, indicate areas of potential strength or weakness, and reveal situations that need further investigation. But financial ratios do not provide answers in and of themselves, and they are not predictive. Financial ratios should be used with considerable caution and common sense; and they should be used in combination with other elements of financial analysis.

It should also be pointed out that there is no one definitive set of key financial ratios; there is no uniform definition for all ratios; there is no standard which should be met for each ratio; and there are no "rules of thumb" that apply to the interpretation of

---

[7] Geoffrey Smith, "Film vs. Digital: Can Kodak Build a Bridge?" *Business Week* (August 2, 1999), p. 66.
[8] Ibid.

financial ratios. Each situation should be evaluated within the context of the particular firm, industry, and economic environment. Finally, it is essential to use the *raw figures* in the financial statements as well as the ratios based on financial statement figures.

Ratios for 5 years, 1996–2000, are provided in each category as background for the comprehensive analysis of Kodak, with the calculation of each ratio shown for the years 1999 and 2000.

Liquidity Ratios: Short-Term Solvency

Eastman Kodak Company	2000	1999	1998	1997	1996	Industry Average 2000
Current ratio	.88	.94	.91	1.06	1.29	1.80
Quick ratio	.61	.68	.68	.82	1.00	.70
Cash flow liquidity	.20	.40	.32	.55	.79	a
Average collection period	69 days	66 days	69 days	57 days	63 days	49 days
Days inventory held	79 days	70 days	72 days	58 days	69 days	139 days
Days payable outstanding	149 days	176 days	196 days	176 days	181 days	34 days
Net trade cycle	(1 day)	(40 days)	(55 days)	(61 days)	(49 days)	154 days
Cash flow from operations (in millions)	982	1,933	1,483	2,080	2,484	a

[a]Not available.

Current Ratio

	2000	1999
$\dfrac{\text{Current assets}}{\text{Current liabilities}}$	$\dfrac{5,491}{6,215} = .88 \text{ times}$	$\dfrac{5,444}{5,769} = .94 \text{ times}$

The current ratio is a commonly used measure of short-run solvency—the ability of a firm to meet its short-term debt requirements as they come due. The available cash resources to satisfy these obligations must come primarily from cash or the conversion to cash of other current assets such as accounts receivable and inventories. As a barometer of short-term liquidity, the current ratio is limited by the nature of its components. Remember that the balance sheet is prepared as of a particular date, and the actual amount of liquid assets may vary considerably from the date on which the balance sheet is prepared. Further, accounts receivable and inventory may not be truly liquid. A firm could have a relatively high current ratio but not be able to meet demands for cash because the accounts receivable are of inferior quality or the inventory is salable only at discounted prices. It is necessary to use other measures of liquidity, including cash flow from operations and additional financial ratios, which rate the liquidity of specific assets, to supplement the current ratio.

The current ratio for Kodak indicates that the current assets do not cover the current liabilities for the firm; the ratio has steadily declined and is below the industry average. Because cash flow from operations has declined over the 5-year period, short-term borrowings have increased. A major reason for the ratio's deteriorating trend is that the steady reduction in Kodak's ability to generate cash from operations has resulted in the need for additional short-term borrowings. The common size balance sheet, shown in Chapter 3, further illustrates the declining proportion of highly liquid assets (cash and cash equivalents) and the increase in short-term borrowings over the 5-year period.

Quick Ratio

	2000	1999
$\dfrac{\text{Current assets } - \text{ inventory}}{\text{Current liabilities}}$	$\dfrac{5,491 - 1,718}{6,215} = .61 \text{ times}$	$\dfrac{5,444 - 1,519}{5,769} = .68 \text{ times}$

The quick ratio is a more rigorous test of short-run solvency than the current ratio because the numerator eliminates inventory, considered the least liquid current asset and the most likely source of losses. The quick ratio for Kodak has declined for the same reasons that the current ratio declined, and also because inventories are significant and rising. Kodak's quick ratio has steadily deteriorated and is below the industry average.

Cash Flow Liquidity Ratio

	2000	1999
$\dfrac{\text{Cash } + \text{ Mkt. Securities } + \text{ CFO}^a}{\text{Current liabilities}}$	$\dfrac{246 + 5 + 982}{6,215} = .20 \text{ times}$	$\dfrac{373 + 20 + 1,933}{5,769} - .40 \text{ times}$

[a]Cash flow from operating activities.

Another approach to measuring short-term solvency is the cash-flow liquidity ratio,[9] which considers cash flow from operating activities (from the statement of cash flows). The cash flow liquidity ratio uses in the numerator (as an approximation of cash resources) cash and marketable securities, which are truly liquid current assets; and cash flow from operating activities, which represents the amount of cash generated from the firm's operations, such as the ability to sell inventory and collect the cash. It is helpful to compare this ratio to the current and quick ratios. Contradictory pictures between this ratio and other liquidity ratios should be investigated thoroughly because, ultimately, companies need cash to pay bills—uncollected accounts receivable and unsold inventory cannot be used to pay bills. High current and quick ratios combined with low or negative cash flow liquidity ratios could signal problems.

The cash flow liquidity ratio for Kodak confirms what has already been seen from the current and quick ratios. The deteriorating cash flow from operations is forcing the company to borrow to cover its bills.

---

[9] For additional reading about this ratio and its applications, see L. Fraser, "Cash Flow from Operations and Liquidity Analysis, A New Financial Ratio for Commercial Lending Decisions," (1989); *Cash Flow*, Robert Morris Associates, Philadelphia, PA. For other cash flow ratios, see C. Carslaw and J. Mills, "Developing Ratios for Effective Cash Flow Statement Analysis," *Journal of Accountancy* (November 1991); D. E. Giacomino and D. E. Mielke, "Cash Flows: Another Approach to Ratio Analysis," *Journal of Accountancy* (March, 1993); and John R. Mills and Jeanne H. Yamamura, "The Power of Cash Flow Ratios," *Journal of Accountancy* (October, 1998).

Average Collection Period

	2000	1999
$\dfrac{\text{Accounts receivable}}{\text{Average daily sales}}$	$\dfrac{2,653}{13,994/365} = 69$ days	$\dfrac{2,537}{14,089/365} = 66$ days

The average collection period for accounts receivable is the average number of days required to convert receivables into cash. This ratio helps gauge the liquidity of accounts receivable—the ability of the firm to collect from customers. It may also provide information about a company's credit policies. For example, if the average collection period is increasing over time or is higher than the industry average, the firm's credit policies could be too lenient and accounts receivable not sufficiently liquid. The loosening of credit could be necessary at times to boost sales, but at an increasing cost to the firm. On the other hand, if credit policies are too restrictive, as reflected in an average collection period that is shortening and less than industry competitors, the firm may be losing qualified customers.

Kodak's collection period has varied between 57 and 69 days over the past 5 years. Of concern is that Kodak is taking about 20 days longer than its competition to collect accounts receivables, indicating credit policies that may be too lenient or receivables that are illiquid. The picture this ratio presents adds to the caution flags already raised about receivables in Chapter 3, where it was noted that accounts receivables for Kodak are increasing while sales (and the allowance for doubtful accounts) are decreasing.

Days Inventory Held

	2000	1999
$\dfrac{\text{Inventory}}{\text{Average daily cost of sales}}$	$\dfrac{1,718}{8,019/365} = 79$ days	$\dfrac{1,519}{7,987/365} = 70$ days

The days inventory held is the average number of days it takes to sell inventory to customers. This ratio measures the efficiency of the firm in managing its inventory. Generally, a low number of days inventory held is a sign of efficient management; the faster inventory sells, the fewer funds are tied up in inventory. However, too low a number could indicate understocking and lost orders, a decrease in prices, a shortage of materials, or more sales than planned. A high number of days inventory held could be the result of carrying too much inventory or stocking inventory that is obsolete, slow-moving, or inferior. On the other hand, there may be legitimate reasons to stockpile inventory, such as increased demand, expansion, or an expected strike.

Kodak's days inventory held, though increasing, is substantially lower than the industry average. A possible reason for the difference with the industry is that the majority of Kodak's sales are from film, whereas the industry average includes competitors whose sales may be largely photographic equipment, an item that would move slower than film. The increasing number of days inventory held compared to prior years indicates that Kodak is less efficient selling inventory than it has been in the past. Like its receivables, Kodak's inventories are rising but sales are declining.

Days Payable Outstanding

	2000	1999
$\dfrac{\text{Accounts payable}}{\text{Average daily cost of sales}}$	$\dfrac{3,275}{8,019/365} = 149\text{ days}$	$\dfrac{3,832}{7,987/365} = 176\text{ days}$

The days payable outstanding is the average number of days the firm takes to pay accounts payable in cash. This ratio offers insight into a firm's pattern of payments to suppliers. An optimal strategy is to delay payment of payables as long as possible but still make payment by the due date in order to avoid finance charges.

Until 2000, Kodak took more than 176 days on average to pay suppliers. In 2000, this number dropped to 149 days, indicating that Kodak is paying its bills sooner. Perhaps Kodak's suppliers tightened their credit policies or there was a change in the mix of products purchased. The effect, though, combined with increases in inventories and receivables, has been that Kodak has had to find other sources of short-term credit for needed operating cash.

Net Trade Cycle

	2000	1999
Average collection period	69 days	66 days
+days inventory held	+ 79 days	+ 70 days
−days payable outstanding	−149 days	−176 days
	(1 day)	(40 days)

The net trade cycle measures the normal cash conversion cycle of a firm—which consists of buying or manufacturing inventory, with some purchases on credit (creation of accounts payable); selling inventory, with some sales on credit (creation of accounts receivable); and collecting cash from accounts receivable. Changes in the net trade cycle help explain why cash flow generation has improved or deteriorated by analyzing the key working capital accounts—accounts receivable, inventory, and accounts payable. The shorter the net trade cycle, the more efficient the firm is in managing its cash.

Kodak's net trade cycle is actually negative, which means that the company is able to sell inventory and collect cash from sales in a shorter period of time than is required to make payments to suppliers. Generally this is a good situation because it should minimize the need for short-term borrowings; but note that Kodak's credit from suppliers, as already discussed, has been greatly reduced in 2000 (the payment period shortened by 27 days), causing Kodak to increase short-term borrowings. This tightening of supplier credit and its effect on the net trade cycle helps explain why the cash flow from operations has dropped from 1999 to 2000—with the firm using cash to pay down payables while lengthening the period over which receivables and inventory are held.

Activity Ratios: Asset Liquidity and Asset Management Efficiency

Eastman Kodak Company	2000	1999	1998	1997	1996	Industry Average 2000
Accounts receivable turnover	5.27	5.55	5.31	6.40	5.83	7.5
Inventory turnover	4.67	5.26	5.12	6.37	5.29	2.6
Payables turnover	2.45	2.08	1.87	2.08	2.02	10.7
Fixed asset turnover	2.36	2.37	2.27	2.64	2.95	11.1
Total asset turnover	.98	.98	.91	1.11	1.11	1.5

Accounts Receivable Turnover

	2000	1999
$\dfrac{\text{Net sales}}{\text{Accounts receivable}}$	$\dfrac{13,994}{2,653} = 5.27\text{x}$	$\dfrac{14,089}{2,537} = 5.55\text{x}$

Inventory Turnover

	2000	1999
$\dfrac{\text{Cost of goods sold}}{\text{Inventory}}$	$\dfrac{8,019}{1,718} = 4.67\text{x}$	$\dfrac{7,987}{1,519} = 5.26\text{x}$

Payables Turnover

	2000	1999
$\dfrac{\text{Cost of goods sold}}{\text{Accounts payable}}$	$\dfrac{8,019}{3,275} = 2.45\text{x}$	$\dfrac{7,987}{3,832} = 2.08\text{x}$

The accounts receivable, inventory, and payables turnover ratios measure how many times, on average, accounts receivable are collected in cash, inventory is sold, and payables are paid during the year. These three measures are mathematical complements to the ratios that make up the net trade cycle, and therefore, measure exactly what the average collection period, days inventory held, and days payable outstanding measure for a firm; they provide an alternative way to look at the same information. As shown in the previous exhibits, Kodak's turnover ratios are lower than the industry average in all areas except inventory management. Although Kodak's inventory turnover is better than the industry, its trend has been declining.

Fixed Asset Turnover

	2000	1999
$\dfrac{\text{Net sales}}{\text{Net property, plant, and equipment}}$	$\dfrac{13,994}{5,919} = 2.36\text{x}$	$\dfrac{14,089}{5,947} = 2.37\text{x}$

Total Asset Turnover

	2000	1999
$\dfrac{\text{Net sales}}{\text{Total assets}}$	$\dfrac{13,994}{14,212} = .98\text{x}$	$\dfrac{14,089}{14,370} = .98\text{x}$

The fixed asset turnover and total asset turnover ratios are two approaches to assessing management's effectiveness in generating sales from investments in assets. The fixed asset turnover considers only the firm's investment in property, plant, and equipment, and is extremely important for a capital-intensive firm, such as a manufacturer with heavy investments in long-lived assets. The total asset turnover measures the efficiency in managing all of a firm's assets. Generally, the higher these ratios, the smaller the investment required to generate sales and thus the more profitable the firm. When the asset turnover ratios are low relative to the industry or the firm's historical record, either the investment in assets is too heavy and/or sales are sluggish. There may, however, be plausible explanations; for example, the firm may have undertaken an extensive plant modernization or placed assets in service at year-end, which will generate positive results in the long-term.

Kodak's fixed and total asset turnover ratios dropped from 1996 to 1998 and then increased slightly in 1999 and 2000, but the overall trend has been downward. Kodak is a capital intensive firm and has over 40 percent of total assets invested in fixed assets. The changes in the fixed asset turnover are a result of increases in fixed assets without a proportional increase in sales (except in 1999, when sales increased and fixed assets decreased).

Leverage Ratios: Debt Financing and Coverage

Eastman Kodak Company	2000	1999	1998	1997	1996	Industry Average 2000
Debt ratio	75.88%	72.78%	72.93%	75.95%	67.21%	55.7%
Long-term debt to total capitalization	25.38%	19.31%	11.22%	15.62	10.56%	a
Debt to equity	3.15	2.67	2.69	3.16	2.05	1.4
Times interest earned	12.44	14.01	17.16	1.33	22.23	2.8
Cash interest coverage	9.84	20.82	23.01	33.06	36.37	a
Fixed charge coverage	7.11	7.51	7.86	1.11	7.08	a
Cash flow adequacy	.40	.66	.51	.58	.71	a

[a]Not available.

Debt Ratio

	2000	1999
$\dfrac{\text{Total liabilities}}{\text{Total assets}}$	$\dfrac{10,784}{14,212} = 75.88\%$	$\dfrac{10,458}{14,370} = 72.78\%$

Long-Term Debt to Total Capitalization

	2000	1999
$\dfrac{\text{Long-term debt}}{\text{Long-term debt + stockholders' equity}}$	$\dfrac{1{,}166}{1{,}166 + 3{,}428} = 25.38\%$	$\dfrac{936}{936 + 3{,}912} = 19.31\%$

Debt to Equity

	2000	1999
$\dfrac{\text{Total liabilities}}{\text{Stockholders' equity}}$	$\dfrac{10{,}784}{3{,}428} = 3.15 \text{ times}$	$\dfrac{10{,}458}{3{,}912} = 2.67 \text{ times}$

Each of the three debt ratios measures the extent of the firm's financing with debt. The amount and proportion of debt in a company's capital structure is important to the financial analyst because of the tradeoff between risk and return. Use of debt involves risk because debt carries a fixed commitment in the form of interest charges and principal repayment. Failure to satisfy the fixed charges associated with debt ultimately results in bankruptcy. A lesser risk is that a firm with too much debt has difficulty obtaining additional debt financing when needed or finds that credit is available only at extremely high rates of interest. Although debt implies risk, it also introduces the potential for increased benefits to the firm's owners. (See the discussion of the return on equity ratio.) An element of debt, which does not show up in these ratios, is off-balance-sheet financing (discussed in Chapter 3). When off-balance-sheet financing exists, the debt ratios do not present the whole picture with regard to risk.

The debt ratio considers the proportion of all assets that are financed with debt. The ratio of long-term debt to total capitalization reveals the extent to which long-term debt is used for the firm's permanent financing (both long-term debt and equity). The debt to equity ratio measures the overall riskiness of the firm's capital structure in terms of the relationship between the funds supplied by creditors (debt) and investors (equity). The higher the proportion of debt, the greater the degree of risk because creditors must be satisfied before owners in the event of bankruptcy. The equity base provides, in effect, a cushion of protection for the suppliers of debt.

Kodak's capital structure is risky when compared to the industry, because the firm has a much higher proportion of debt than its competitors. The debt ratios reflect Kodak's increased use of both short-term and long-term borrowings. The company has had to borrow more due in large part to the decreasing cash flow from operations. Adding to the risk are the commitments Kodak has that are not even included in the above ratios, but must be discovered by reading the notes. As discussed in Chapter 3 and shown in Note 8 to the financial statements, Kodak has commitments of at least $1,668 million.

Times Interest Earned

	2000	1999
$\dfrac{\text{Operating profit}}{\text{Interest expense}}$	$\dfrac{2{,}214}{178} = 12.44 \text{ times}$	$\dfrac{1{,}990}{142} = 14.01 \text{ times}$

Cash Interest Coverage

	2000	1999
$\dfrac{\text{CFO} + \text{interest paid} + \text{taxes paid}^a}{\text{Interest paid}}$	$\dfrac{982 + 166 + 486}{166} = 9.84 \text{ times}$	$\dfrac{1,933 + 120 + 445}{120} = 20.82 \text{ times}$

[a]The amounts for interest paid and taxes paid are found in the supplemental disclosures on the statement of cash flows.

In order for a firm to benefit from debt financing, the fixed interest payments that accompany debt must be more than satisfied from operating earnings.[10] Generally, the higher the times interest earned ratio, the better the firm's situation; however, if a company is generating high profits but no cash flow from operations, this ratio is misleading. It takes cash to make interest payments! The cash interest coverage ratio measures how many times interest payments can be covered by cash flow from operations before interest and taxes.

Kodak's shareholders are benefiting from the use of debt (through financial leverage). Kodak does better than the industry; however, note that in 2000 both these ratios declined, a result of higher interest and less cash generated from operations.

Fixed Charge Coverage

	2000	1999
$\dfrac{\text{Operating profit} + \text{rent expense}}{\text{Interest expense} + \text{rent expense}}$	$\dfrac{2,214 + 155}{178 + 155} = 7.11 \text{ times}$	$\dfrac{1,990 + 142}{142 + 142} = 7.51 \text{ times}$

The fixed charge coverage ratio is a broader measure of coverage capability than the times interest earned ratio because it includes the fixed payments associated with operating leases. Lease payments, more commonly referred to as rent expense in the notes, are added back in the numerator because they were deducted as an operating expense to calculate operating profit. Lease payments are similar in nature to interest expense in that they both represent obligations that must be met on an annual basis. The fixed charge coverage ratio is important for firms that operate extensively with operating leases.

Kodak is able to cover fixed charges with operating profits, but the ratio has decreased in 2000, as a result of increased rent and interest expense.

Cash Flow Adequacy

	2000	1999
$\dfrac{\text{CFO}}{\text{Capital expenditures} + \text{debt repayments} + \text{dividends paid}}$	$\dfrac{982}{945 + 936 + 545} = .40 \text{ times}$	$\dfrac{1,933}{1,127 + 1,254 + 563} = .66 \text{ times}$

---

[10] The operating return, operating profit divided by assets, must exceed the cost of debt, interest expense divided by liabilities.

The cash flow adequacy ratio measures how well a company can cover annual payments of items such as debt, capital expenditures, and dividends from operating cash flow. Cash flow adequacy is generally defined differently by analysts and credit rating agencies; therefore, it is important to understand what is actually being measured. For example, this ratio could be adjusted to include only debt, both debt and lease payments, or any other combination of items the analyst deemed necessary to evaluate the adequacy of cash to meet the firm's needs. It is desirable for companies to generate enough cash flow from operations to cover repayments of debt, some new capital expenditures, and any cash dividends paid.

Kodak's cash has not covered these items in any of the past 5 years. This means Kodak is forced to borrow, or find other means to cover these payments. Although Kodak has reduced debt repayments, fixed asset purchases, and dividends, cash generated from operations dropped almost in half from 1999 to 2000.

Profitability Ratios: Overall Efficiency and Performance

Eastman Kodak Company	2000	1999	1998	1997	1996	Industry Average 2000
Gross profit margin	42.70%	43.31%	45.60%	45.14%	47.85%	36.8%
Operating profit margin	15.82%	14.12%	14.08%	.89%	11.55%	4.1%
Net profit margin	10.05%	9.88%	10.37%	.03%	8.07%	a
Cash flow margin	7.02%	13.72%	11.06%	14.31%	15.56%	a
Return on assets	9.90%	9.69%	9.43%	.04%	8.92%	a
Return on equity	41.04%	35.58%	34.85%	.16%	27.21%	a
Cash return on assets	6.91%	13.45%	10.07%	15.82%	17.20%	a

[a]Not available.

Gross Profit Margin

	2000	1999
$\dfrac{\text{Gross profit}}{\text{Net sales}}$	$\dfrac{5,975}{13,994} = 42.70\%$	$\dfrac{6,102}{14,089} = 43.31\%$

Operating Profit Margin

	2000	1999
$\dfrac{\text{Operating profit}}{\text{Net sales}}$	$\dfrac{2,214}{13,994} = 15.82\%$	$\dfrac{1,990}{14,089} = 14.12\%$

Net Profit Margin

	2000	1999
$\dfrac{\text{Net profit}}{\text{Net sales}}$	$\dfrac{1,407}{13,994} = 10.05\%$	$\dfrac{1,392}{14,089} = 9.88\%$

Gross profit margin, operating profit margin, and net profit margin represent the firm's ability to translate sales dollars into profits at different stages of measurement. The gross profit margin, which shows the relationship between sales and the cost of products sold, measures the ability of a company both to control costs of inventories or manufacturing of products and to pass along price increases through sales to customers. The operating profit margin, a measure of overall operating efficiency, incorporates all of the expenses associated with ordinary business activities. The net profit margin measures profitability after consideration of all revenue and expense, including interest, taxes, and nonoperating items.

Kodak's gross and operating profit margins are better than the industry averages. Of concern is the declining gross profit margin which, according to the management's discussion and analysis, is the result of lower selling prices and increased sales of lower margin products. Operating profit margin has improved, despite the decline in gross profit margin. This was accomplished through a restructuring program that resulted in cost reductions. As discussed in Chapter 2, firms must be careful not to reduce needed expenditures in research and development and advertising too much, or sales and market share may ultimately be hurt. If Kodak has in fact reduced these expenditures without impacting necessary research and advertising, this is a positive move.

The net profit margin has been positively impacted by the reduction of operating costs, but negatively impacted by the increased interest expense caused by higher borrowing, higher interest rates, and the gradual decline of other income.

Cash Flow Margin

	2000	1999
$\dfrac{\text{CFO}}{\text{Net sales}}$	$\dfrac{982}{13,994} = 7.02\%$	$\dfrac{1,933}{14,089} = 13.72\%$

Another important perspective on operating performance is the relationship between cash generated from operations and sales. As pointed out in Chapter 4, it is cash, not accrual-measured earnings, that a firm needs to service debt, pay dividends, and invest in new capital assets. The cash flow margin measures the ability of the firm to translate sales into cash.

Kodak's cash flow from operations has dropped significantly in 2000 and this has affected the cash flow margin ratio. It is obviously important for Kodak to consider ways to improve operating cash flow.

Return on Assets (ROA) or Return on Investment (ROI)

	2000	1999
$\dfrac{\text{Net profit}}{\text{Total assets}}$	$\dfrac{1,407}{14,212} = 9.90\%$	$\dfrac{1,392}{14,370} = 9.69\%$

BOX 5-1
Financial Leverage: An Illustration

Assume that a company has $100,000 in total assets, with a capital structure of 50 percent ($50,000) debt and 50 percent ($50,000) equity, a 10 percent cost of debt, and 40 percent average tax rate.

If the company's operating earnings are $25,000, the return on equity would be calculated as follows:

Operating earnings	$25,000
Interest expense ($50,000 × .10)	5,000
Earnings before tax	$20,000
Tax expense ($20,000 × .40)	8,000
Net earnings	$12,000
Return on equity	12,000/50,000 = 24%

If operating earnings double to $50,000, the return on equity more than doubles (from 24 percent to 54 percent):

Operating earnings	$50,000
Interest expense ($50,000 × .10)	5,000
Earnings before tax	$45,000
Income tax expense ($45,000 × .40)	18,000
Net earnings	$27,000
Return on equity	27,000/50,000 = 54%

On the other hand, if operating earnings are reduced in half to $12,500, the return on equity falls by more than half (from 24 percent to 9 percent):

Operating earnings	$12,500
Interest expense ($50,000 × .10)	5,000
Earnings before tax	$ 7,500
Income tax expense ($7,500 × .40)	3,000
Net earnings	$ 4,500
Return on equity	4,500/50,000 = 9%

Return on Equity (ROE)

	2000	1999
Net profit / Stockholders' equity	$\dfrac{1,407}{3,428} = 41.04\%$	$\dfrac{1,392}{3,912} = 35.58\%$

Return on assets and return on equity are two ratios that measure the overall efficiency of the firm in managing its total investment in assets and in generating return to shareholders. Return on investment or return on assets indicates the amount of profit earned relative to the level of investment in total assets. Return on equity measures the return to common shareholders; this ratio is also calculated as return on common equity if a firm has preferred stock outstanding.

Kodak's ROA and ROE ratios have both improved as a result of the decreased operating costs. The reason for the high return on equity relates to the concept of financial leverage. If a firm earns more than the after-tax cost of debt, shareholders benefit because each dollar earned after covering interest charges is a dollar that is returned to the owners of the firm, rather than being paid to creditors. The greater the proportion of debt in the capital structure, the greater is the potential return to shareholders, and returns are magnified by financial leverage. Because of the risk associated with debt (the fixed payments on debt that must be met) financial leverage has a double edge, as shown in Box 5-1. The amount of interest expense is fixed, regardless of the level of operating earnings. When operating earnings rise or fall, financial leverage produces positive or negative effects on shareholder returns. In evaluating a firm's capital structure, the analyst must weigh the potential benefits of debt against the inherent risk.

Kodak has benefited from the use of financial leverage in recent years with high and increasing returns on equity. The disadvantage of debt, however, is illustrated by Kodak's performance in 1997, when operating returns fell substantially, and the overall return on equity dropped to less than 1 percent.

Cash Return on Assets

	2000	1999
$\dfrac{\text{CFO}}{\text{Total assets}}$	$\dfrac{982}{14,212} = 6.91\%$	$\dfrac{1,933}{14,370} = 13.45\%$

The cash return on assets offers a useful comparison to return on assets. Again, the relationship between cash generated from operations and an accrual-based number allows the analyst to measure the firm's cash-generating ability of assets. Cash is required for future investments. Kodak's cash return on assets has declined in 2000 due to the drop in cash generated from operations.

Market Ratios

Although a sophisticated investment analysis is beyond the scope of this book, we include several commonly used market ratios that may be of interest to investors. Kodak's basic and fully diluted **earnings per common share** were discussed in Chapter 2. The **dividend yield** relates cash dividends to the firm's market price. Kodak's dividend yield, based on cash dividends in 2000 of $1.76 per share and a year-end stock price of $39, was 4.5 percent ($1.76/$39).

The **price-to-earnings ratio** relates earnings per common share to the market price at which the stock trades, expressing the "multiple" which the stock market places on a firm's earnings. Kodak's basic earnings per share were $4.62 for the year 2000, and the stock closed at $39 per share at year-end 2000, which means that the price-to-earnings ratio was 8.4 ($39/$4.62). One of Kodak's competitors, Canon Inc., had basic earnings per share of $1.16 in 2000 with a year-end stock price of $34 and a price-to-earnings ratio of 29.3 ($34/$1.16), which means that the market placed a much higher "multiple" on Canon's reported earnings than on Kodak's. There are a multitude of reasons relating to such issues as risk, uncertainty, and earnings quality for why investors value one firm's earnings higher than another's in estimating future potential. But some answers are suggested by considering the same set of financial ratios for Kodak and Canon (see Exhibit 5–1).

In spite of better profitability and return measures, Kodak is clearly less liquid than Canon and generated a lower amount of operating cash flow. Overall asset management was the same for both companies. These ratios between Kodak and Canon provide anecdotal evidence of the importance being placed by investors on cash flow from operations relative to earnings. The areas in which Kodak tops Canon—inventory management, profitability ratios, and return on assets and equity—are more than offset by Canon's performance in producing cash from operations, which shows up in the cash flow liquidity, cash interest coverage, cash flow adequacy, and cash return on assets ratios.

Exhibit 5-1

Financial Ratio Comparison: Kodak and Canon

FINANCIAL RATIOS (2000)	KODAK	CANON
Liquidity		
Current (times)	.88	1.71
Quick (times)	.61	1.21
Cash flow liquidity (times)	.20	.87
Cash flow from operations (in millions of dollars)	982	2,610
Activity		
Accounts receivable turnover (times)	5.27	5.80
Inventory turnover (times)	4.67	3.21
Payables turnover (times)	2.45	3.55
Fixed asset turnover (times)	2.36	3.60
Total asset turnover (times)	.98	.98
Leverage		
Debt ratio (%)	75.88	54.13
Times interest earned (times)	12.44	16.39
Cash interest coverage (times)	9.84	30.39
Cash flow adequacy (times)	.40	1.29
Profitability		
Gross profit margin (%)	42.70	43.28
Operating profit margin (%)	15.82	8.84
Net profit margin (%)	10.05	4.82
Cash flow margin (%)	7.02	12.46
Return on assets (%)	9.90	4.73
Return on equity (%)	41.04	10.33
Cash return on assets (%)	6.91	12.24

Ratio Summary

Figure 5-1 summarizes the use of key financial ratios discussed in this chapter. This chart can be especially helpful in selecting what ratios to use to meet a particular analytical objective.

Segment Information

Companies that have substantial operations outside of the United States or operate in unrelated lines of business are required to report financial information about these operations as supplementary schedules in the annual report. These disclosures are useful in analysis by helping identify areas of strength and weakness within a company, the proportionate contribution to revenue and profit by divisions, and the relationship between capital expenditures and rates of return by operating areas. Based on these supplementary disclosures, some summary ratios are provided on Kodak's segmental and geographic operations.

Figure 5-1
How to use financial ratios

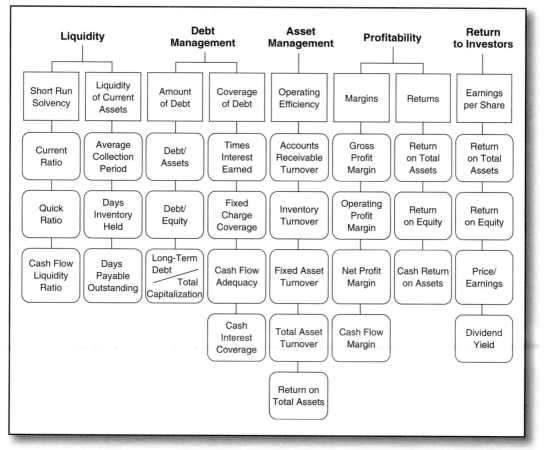

Contribution by Segment to Capital Expenditures (Percentages)	2000	1999	1998
Consumer Imaging	53.7	64.3	56.2
Kodak Professional	13.0	13.0	12.9
Health Imaging	12.7	8.2	7.9
Other Imaging	20.6	14.5	23.0
Total Sales	100.0	100.0	100.0

Contribution by Segment to Operating Profit (Percentages)	2000	1999	1998
Consumer Imaging	54.3	55.5	57.2
Kodak Professional	12.0	16.0	17.5
Health Imaging	23.2	20.1	17.0
Other Imaging	10.5	8.4	8.3
Total Sales	100.0	100.0	100.0

Return on Investment by Segment (Percentages)	2000	1999	1998
Consumer Imaging	16.6	18.0	16.2
Kodak Professional	7.3	16.2	14.9
Health Imaging	23.4	25.6	18.1
Other Imaging	12.0	20.7	13.8

Kodak's strategy, as evidenced by capital expenditures by segment, appears to be a reduced focus (no pun intended) in the "Consumer Imaging" segment and expansion in "Health Imaging" segments. Consideration of segment profit information offers insight as to the effectiveness of this strategy. The proportion of operating profit contributed by the "Health Imaging" segment has steadily risen, whereas the contributions of "Consumer Imaging" and "Kodak Professional" have declined. Although the "Other Imaging" segment also appears promising, the management discussion and analysis section discloses that special items have skewed the results for this segment, and it did not actually improve.

Overall return on investment shows clear deterioration in the Kodak "Professional" segment, reasonable stability in "Consumer Imaging," overall improvement in "Health Imaging" with some decline in 2000, and a bumpy path for "Other Imaging." The "Health Imaging" segment appears to be the most promising segment for Kodak, generating the highest returns on investment. The "Other Imaging" unit has volatile returns. This unit is dependent on the entertainment industry and government, and may be more affected by changes in the economic climate than the "Health Imaging" area.

Contribution by Segment to Sales (Percentages)	2000	1999	1998
United States	48.6	47.7	47.9
Europe, Middle East, and Africa	24.7	26.5	27.6
Asia Pacific	16.8	16.1	15.0
Canada and Latin America	9.9	9.7	9.5
Total Sales	100.0	100.0	100.0

Long-Lived Assets by Segment (Percentages)	2000	1999	1998
United States	66.1	65.7	68.4
Europe, Middle East, and Africa	10.9	12.0	14.5
Asia Pacific	17.9	17.2	11.9
Canada and Latin America	5.1	5.1	5.2
Total Assets	100.0	100.0	100.0

The exhibit showing contribution to sales by geographic regions reveals that more than half of Kodak's sales are in foreign markets, although the proportion of sales in the United States rose slightly in 2000. Revenues in Asia Pacific have gradually gained ground relative to markets in Europe, the Middle East, and Africa. Comparing these percentages to the percentage of long-lived assets in each geographic location offers a possible reason for this trend. The proportion of investments in assets in Europe, the Middle East, and Africa has declined, an indication that operations may have been downsized in favor of increases in the Asia Pacific region.

Summary of Analysis

A comprehensive analysis of any company's financial reports encompasses many steps and interrelated pieces. No one part of the analysis should be interpreted in isolation from the other parts. The firm's ability to generate cash from operations determines its borrowing needs. The amount of debt affects both risk and return.

Short-term liquidity impacts profitability, which begins with sales. Sales are dependent upon receivables and inventory management, which relate to liquidity. The efficiency of asset management influences the cost and availability of credit, which shapes the capital structure and overall returns. Every aspect of a company's financial condition, operating performance, and outlook influences the share price.

The final step in a comprehensive analysis is to integrate the separate pieces of the analysis, leading to overall conclusions about the firm's financial health and prospects. The specific conclusions reached are affected by the objectives established and the questions raised at the beginning of the analytical process. The major findings from the comprehensive analysis of Kodak's financial statements are summarized by the following strengths and weaknesses.

Strengths

Successful use of financial leverage (debt)
Fixed charge coverage stable
Operating profit strong
Overall improvement in return on assets and equity
Cost savings through restructuring programs
Profitability of picture-making kiosks at retail stores
Productive growth in "Health Imaging" segment
Geographic diversity

Weaknesses

Change at top, new CEO (could also be strength)
Declining sales and gross profit
Lack of profitability on digital cameras
Economic outlook not promising
"Big Bath" write-offs in 1999 affect comparability
Decreasing cash flow from operations
Increasing borrowing needs
Liquidity trending downward
Accounts receivable and inventory growing faster than sales
Overall asset management trending downward
Price to earnings ratio low relative to competition
Deterioration in cash interest coverage, cash flow adequacy, cash flow margin, and cash return on assets
Volatile returns in "Other Imaging" segment and decreasing returns in Kodak "Professional" segment

The overall evaluation of Kodak depends considerably on the values one places on each area of strength and weakness. Kodak's declining stock price indicates more weight is being given to weaknesses than to strengths by investors, but Kodak has had no difficulty accessing funds through borrowings. The economic outlook is not helpful to the many areas of Kodak's operations that are sensitive to economic downturns. On the other hand, a prospective employee might be drawn to Kodak for the considerable challenges the company offers.

This comprehensive analysis of Kodak, however, is not provided to help readers decide whether to invest in, lend money to, or go to work for Kodak. Rather, the

Kodak discussion is intended as an illustration of how to analyze any company's financial statements and to contribute to the overall objective of this book, which is to help readers rely on their own understanding and interpretation of the material in a corporate annual report in making important financial decisions.

READERS' CHECKLIST OF CAUTION FLAGS FROM CHAPTER 5

- ➤ Changes in top company management
- ➤ Key financial ratios indicating deteriorating trends and/or weaknesses relative to industry competitors
- ➤ Cash flow from operations declining, negative, volatile, or not tracking with net income
- ➤ Lack of profitability in key operating areas
- ➤ Price to earnings ratio low relative to competitors

- ➤ Firm's earnings less than after-tax cost of debt
- ➤ Declining operating profits when debt is rising
- ➤ Deteriorating trends in operating segments
- ➤ Assuming the authors are wealthy because they always make wise business decisions

TEST YOURSELF

Solutions are provided immediately following the Glossary at the end of the book.

1. What is an investor's objective in financial statement analysis?
   a. To determine the company's strategies
   b. To determine the future potential and value of the company
   c. To calculate financial ratios
   d. To determine if the company has been profitable in the past
2. What is a creditor's objective in financial statement analysis?
   a. To determine if the accrual basis of accounting will allow for payment of debt
   b. To determine if the company's strategies were accomplished
   c. To assess the company's ability to meet cash needs as they arise
   d. To assess how the firm operates compared to its competitors
3. Which of the following are sources of information when evaluating a firm's financial condition?
   a. Form 10-K and Form 10-Q
   b. Proxy statement
   c. Current periodical articles about the firm
   d. All of the above
4. Which tool or technique would not be useful in a financial analysis of a firm?
   a. Industry comparisons
   b. Financial ratios
   c. A "big bathtub"
   d. Common sense and judgment
5. What do liquidity ratios measure?
   a. The extent of a firm's financing with debt
   b. The firm's ability to meet cash needs as they arise

c. The firm's efficiency in managing assets

d. None of the above

6. What is a limitation of the current ratio?
    a. A high current ratio can be misleading if accounts receivable are of inferior quality and the inventory is not salable.
    b. The current ratio does not include inventory in its numerator because it is the least liquid of the current assets.
    c. The current ratio has no limitations.
    d. Both (a) and (b)

7. Which ratio helps assess the receivables account and credit policies of a company?
    a. Quick ratio
    b. Cash flow liquidity ratio
    c. Days inventory held
    d. Average collection period

8. What does an increasing collection period for receivables suggest about a firm's credit policy?
    a. The credit policy may be too lenient.
    b. The credit policy may be too restrictive.
    c. The credit policy has nothing to do with the collection period.
    d. Sales may be declining.

9. What does the net trade cycle measure for a firm?
    a. The number of days that inventory is held per year
    b. The average collection period plus the days inventory held minus the days payable outstanding
    c. The normal cash conversion cycle of a firm
    d. Both (b) and (c)

10. Which three ratios are mathematical complements to the ratios that make up the net trade cycle?
    a. Current ratio, quick ratio, cash flow liquidity ratio
    b. Gross profit margin, operating profit margin, net profit margin
    c. Average collection period, days inventory held, days payable outstanding
    d. Accounts receivable turnover, inventory turnover, payables turnover

11. What causes the asset turnover ratios to be too low?
    a. Too large an investment in assets or sluggish sales
    b. Downsizing
    c. Too small an investment in assets and robust sales
    d. High profitability

12. Why is debt risky?
    a. Debt is not risky.
    b. Debt carries a fixed commitment in the form of interest charges and principal repayment.
    c. Debt is an off-balance-sheet item.
    d. Owners are satisfied before creditors in the case of bankruptcy.

13. When is it important to calculate the fixed charge coverage ratio?
    a. If the firm has capital leases, but not operating leases
    b. If the firm has depreciation and amortization expense
    c. If the firm has interest expense and operating lease payments
    d. If the firm has interest expense and interest income

14. Which of the following statements is false?
    a. When off-balance-sheet financing exists, the debt ratios do not present the whole picture with regard to risk.
    b. Although debt implies risk, it also introduces the potential for increased benefits to the firm's owners.
    c. Times interest earned measures how many times interest payments can be covered by cash flow from operations.
    d. Cash flow adequacy is generally defined differently by analysts and credit rating agencies.
15. What does the gross profit margin measure?
    a. The relationship between sales and cost of goods sold
    b. The ability of a firm to control costs of inventory
    c. The ability of the firm to pass along price increases through sales to customers
    d. All of the above
16. Why is it important to calculate ratios that include cash flow in the calculation?
    a. It is cash, not accrual measured earnings, that a firm needs to pay for debt, dividends, operating expenses, and purchases of capital assets.
    b. Cash flow ratios are only useful to creditors; investors do not need to calculate these ratios.
    c. It is only important to calculate ratios that include cash flow if the cash flow from operations is a negative number.
    d. None of the above
17. Which ratios measure the overall efficiency of the firm in managing its investment in assets and generating return to shareholders?
    a. Debt to equity and net profit margin
    b. Cash return on assets and average collection period
    c. Return on investment and return on equity
    d. Net trade cycle and cash conversion cycle
18. How does financial leverage benefit shareholders?
    a. The greater the equity relative to debt, the less chance there is for bankruptcy.
    b. The greater the proportion of debt in the capital structure, the greater is the potential return to shareholders, if a firm earns more than the after-tax cost of debt.
    c. The greater the operating earnings the greater is the interest expense that can be deducted for tax purposes.
    d. If preferred stock is greater than common stock, then earnings are spread over fewer shares of stock.
19. What does the price-to-earnings ratio measure?
    a. The "multiple" that the stock market places on a firm's earnings
    b. The amount of earnings for each share of stock outstanding
    c. The relationship of cash dividends to the firm's market price
    d. The profitability of the firm
20. How can segment information be helpful when evaluating the financial condition of a firm?
    a. These disclosures highlight global concerns such as the effects of foreign currency translation.
    b. These disclosures help assess the risk and return of geographic segments.
    c. These disclosures help identify strengths and weaknesses within a company by evaluating the contribution to revenue and profit by divisions.
    d. These disclosures help assess the relationship between capital expenditures and the market price for the firm's stock.

Supplement

Caution Flags and WorldCom, Inc.

As *Understanding the Corporate Annual Report: Nuts, Bolts, and a Few Loose Screws* was in the final stages of production, news emerged about the financial crisis of the telecommunications company WorldCom, Inc. The Securities and Exchange Commission has filed charges against WorldCom, Inc., for falsely reporting profits of $3.8 billion in 2001 and 2002 as the result of inappropriately capitalizing expenses (spreading the costs out over several years rather than recognizing the expenses in the year they occurred). The charges against WorldCom, Inc., appear to represent the largest case of accounting fraud in U.S. history.

The obvious question for readers of this book is whether the information presented—and especially the caution flags raised—throughout these chapters would have been helpful to investors, creditors, and employees in signaling the problems at WorldCom, Inc., announced in June 2002. Specifically, what clues would readers find in the 2001 WorldCom, Inc., corporate annual report, given that the problems involve accounting fraud that is not detectable by readers of an annual report (or even their accountants#!x)?

As detailed in Chapter 2, companies that are manipulating their financial reports with creative accounting usually have one or more caution flags emitting signals. The caution flags discussed in this book relate to *items that can be readily identified* by readers of a firm's annual report. Although they do not explain a problem or even confirm that one exists, they provide clues that the company may have financial difficulties. They also signal the need to dig deeper, especially when there are multiple caution flags raised in one set of financial statements and notes.

There are numerous caution flags in the *2001 Annual Report for WorldCom, Inc.* Provided here are some of the more dramatic examples (based on the financial statements as originally reported, prior to the required restatement).

➢ **Caution Flag:** Revenue and earnings moving at different rates or in opposite directions (Chapters 1 and 2).

• WorldCom, Inc.: Between 2000 and 2001, revenue declined by **10 percent** (from $39,090 million to $35,179 million), while earnings fell by **64 percent** (from $4,153 million to $1,501 million). *Source:* Consolidated Statements of Operations.

➢ **Caution Flag:** Net income and cash flow from operations moving in different directions (Chapter 4).

• WorldCom, Inc.:

	Change in Net Income	Change in Cash Flow from Operations
1999–2000	**+3%**	**-30%**
2000–2001	**-64%**	**+4%**

Source: Consolidated Statements of Operations and Consolidated Statements of Cash Flows.

➤ **Caution Flag:** Write-down in value of goodwill (Chapter 3).

• WorldCom, Inc.: "Based on our preliminary estimates, we estimate that as a result of the adoption of SFAS 142 we will reduce goodwill by $15 billion to $20 billion. . . ."
Source: Note 1, "The Company and Significant Accounting Policies—Recently Issued Accounting Standards."

➤ **Caution Flag:** Borrowings growing faster than assets being financed (Chapter 3).

• WorldCom, Inc.: Between 2000 and 2001, net property, plant, and equipment increased by **4 percent** (from $37,423 million to $38,809 million) while long-term debt rose by **70 percent** (from $17,696 million to $30,038 million).
Source: Consolidated Balance Sheets.

➤ **Caution Flag:** Declining operating income when debt is rising (Chapter 5).

• WorldCom, Inc.: Between 2000 and 2001, operating income decreased by **57 percent,** total liabilities rose by **9 percent,** and long-term debt rose by **70 percent.** As a result, return on equity declined by **68 percent** between 2000 and 2001, dropping from **7.4 percent** to **2.4 percent.**
Source: Consolidated Statements of Operations and Consolidated Balance Sheets.

➤ **Caution Flag:** Departure from "unqualified" opinion in the auditor's report with "exception, or explanatory" language or qualification (Chapter 1).

• WorldCom, Inc.: "As discussed in Note 1 to the consolidated financial statements, effective January 1, 2000, the Company changed its method of accounting for certain activations and installation fee revenues and expenses."
Source: Report of Independent Public Accountants (Arthur Andersen LLP).

➤ **Caution Flag:** Company puts name on sports arena (Chapter 1).

• WorldCom, Inc.: "Worldcom, Inc.'s, financial crisis . . . may even force the MCI Center in Washington to be renamed, sports marketers said."
Source: John Porretto, "WorldCom Crisis," Associated Press, printed in *Arizona Republic,* June 27, 2002, D6. (MCI is an integrated business of WorldCom, Inc.) Author's note: This is the only caution flag that did not appear in the *2001 Annual Report for WorldCom, Inc.*

These examples do not identify the overstatement of earnings by WorldCom, Inc., that led to the charges filed by the SEC. What they show is a pattern in the firm's financial performance and financial reporting that raises serious questions about the company's financial condition and identifies specific areas that require further analysis. A company uses manipulative accounting practices in order to *appear* to be performing better than it actually is and/or to *hide* financial problems, both of which unfortunately turned out to be the situation for WorldCom, Inc. The authors hope that, in the future, there will be fewer and fewer such real-world tests of the material presented in this book, but that readers will be well prepared for those they do encounter.

GLOSSARY

Accounts payable Amounts owed to creditors for items or services purchased from them.

Accounts receivable Amounts owed to an entity, primarily by its trade customers.

Accounts receivable turnover Indicates how many times receivables are collected during a year, on average.

Accrual basis of accounting A method of earnings determination under which revenues are recognized in the accounting period when earned, regardless of when cash is received; and expenses are recognized in the period incurred, regardless of when cash is paid.

Accumulated depreciation A balance sheet account indicating the amount of depreciation expense taken on plant and equipment up to the balance sheet date.

Accumulated other comprehensive income or loss An account that includes unrealized gains or losses in the market value of investments of marketable securities classified as available for sale, specific types of pension liability adjustments, certain gains and losses on derivative financial instruments, and foreign currency translation adjustments resulting when financial statements from a foreign currency are converted into U.S. dollars.

Activity ratio A ratio that measures the liquidity of specific assets and the efficiency of the firm in managing assets.

Additional paid-in-capital The amount by which the original sales price of stock shares sold exceeds the par value of the stock.

Adverse opinion Opinion rendered by an independent auditor stating that the financial statements have not been presented fairly in accordance with generally accepted accounting principles.

Advertising expense Cost associated with marketing a product or service.

Allowance for doubtful accounts The balance sheet account that measures the amount of outstanding accounts receivable expected to be uncollectable.

Amortization The process of expense allocation applied to the cost expiration of intangible assets.

Annual pension cost or income The income (loss) recognized if the expected return on pension assets exceeds the cost (is less than the cost) of pension benefits.

Annual report The report to shareholders published by a firm; contains information required by generally accepted accounting principles and/or by specific Securities and Exchange Commission requirements.

Assets Items possessing service or use potential to owner.

Auditor's report Report by independent auditor attesting to the fairness of the financial statements of a company.

Average collection period Indicates days required to convert receivables into cash.

Average cost method A method of valuing inventory and cost of products sold; all costs, including those in beginning inventory, are added together and divided by the total number of units to arrive at a cost per unit.

Balance sheet The financial statement that shows the financial condition of a company on a particular date.

Balancing equation Assets = Liabilities + Shareholders' Equity.

Barter   The recording of revenues on deals not including cash.

Basic earnings per share   The earnings per share figure calculated by dividing net earnings available to common shareholders by the average number of common shares outstanding.

Big bath   Enormous write-offs taken in one period.

Calendar year   The year starting January 1 and ending December 31.

Capital assets   *See* Fixed assets.

Capital in excess of par value   *See* Additional paid-in-capital.

Capital lease   A leasing arrangement that is, in substance, a purchase by the lessee, who accounts for the lease as an acquisition of an asset and the incurrence of a liability.

Capital structure   The permanent long-term financing of a firm represented by long-term debt, preferred stock, common stock, and retained earnings.

Cash basis of accounting   A method of accounting under which revenues are recorded when cash is received and expenses are recognized when cash is paid.

Cash conversion cycle   The amount of time (expressed in number of days) required to sell inventory and collect accounts receivable, less the number of days credit extended by suppliers.

Cash equivalents   Security investments that are readily converted to cash.

Cash flow adequacy   Measures how many times average annual payments of long-term debt are covered by operating cash flow.

Cash flow from financing activities   On the statement of cash flows, cash generated from/used by financing activities.

Cash flow from investing activities   On the statement of cash flows, cash generated from/used by investing activities.

Cash flow from operating activities   On the statement of cash flows, cash generated/used by operating activities.

Cash flow from operations   The amount of cash generated from/used by a business enterprise's normal, ongoing operations during an accounting period.

Cash flow liquidity ratio   Measures short-term liquidity by considering as cash resources (numerator) cash plus cash equivalents plus cash flow from operating activities.

Cash flow margin   Measures the ability of the firm to generate cash from sales.

Cash interest coverage   Measures how many times interest payments can be covered by cash flow from operations before interest and taxes.

Cash return on assets   Measures the return on assets on a cash basis.

Channel stuffing   A practice used to encourage customers to purchase more products than they need or goods they are not ready to buy.

Commercial paper   Unsecured promissory notes of large companies.

Commitments   Contractual agreements that will have a significant impact on the company in the future.

Common size financial statements   A form of financial ratio analysis that allows the comparison of firms with different levels of sales or total assets by introducing a common denominator. A common size balance sheet expresses each item on the balance sheet as a percentage of total assets, and a common size income statement expresses each item as a percentage of net sales.

Common stock   Shares of stock representing ownership in a company.

Complex capital structure   Capital structures including convertible securities, stock options, and warrants.

Comprehensive income or loss *See* Accumulated other comprehensive income or loss.

Conservatism   The accounting concept that when selecting among accounting methods the choice should be the one with the least favorable effect on the firm.

Consolidated statement of earnings   *See* Income statement.

Consolidated statement of financial position *See* Balance sheet.

Consolidated statement of shareholders' equity   *See* Statement of shareholders' equity.

Consolidation   The combination of financial statements for two or more separate legal entities when one company, the parent, owns more than 50 percent of the voting stock of the other company or companies.

Contingencies   Potential liabilities of a company.

Convertible securities Securities that can be converted or exchanged for another type of security, typically common stock.

Core earnings *See* Pro forma earnings.

Cost flow assumption An assumption regarding the order in which inventory is sold; used to value cost of goods sold and ending inventory.

Cost method A procedure to account for investments in the voting stock of other companies under which the investor recognizes investment income only to the extent of any cash dividends received.

Cost of goods sold The cost to the seller of products sold to customers.

Cost of sales *See* Cost of goods sold.

Creditor Someone to whom a debt is owing.

Cumulative effect of change in accounting principle The difference in the actual amount of retained earnings at the beginning of the period in which a change in accounting principle is instituted and the amount of retained earnings that would have been reported at that date if the new accounting principle had been applied retroactively for all prior periods.

Current (assets/liabilities) Items expected to be converted into cash or paid out in cash in one year or one operating cycle, whichever is longer.

Current maturities of long-term debt The portion of long-term debt that will be repaid during the upcoming year.

Current ratio Measures short-term liquidity, the ability of a firm to meet needs for cash as they arise.

Days inventory held Measures the average number of days it takes to sell inventory to customers.

Days payable outstanding Measures the average number of days the firm takes to pay accounts payable in cash.

Debt ratio Shows proportion of all assets that are financed with debt.

Debt to equity ratio Measures debt relative to equity base.

Deferred taxes The balance sheet account that results from temporary differences in the recognition of revenue and expense for taxable income and reported income.

Defined benefit pension plan A pension plan in which the employer specifies the amount that will be paid to employees after retirement.

Defined contribution pension plan A pension plan in which the employer specifies the amount contributed to the plan for the employee.

Depletion The accounting procedure used to allocate the cost of acquiring and developing natural resources.

Depreciation The accounting procedure used to allocate the cost of an asset that will benefit a business enterprise for more than a year over the asset's service life.

Derivatives Financial instruments that derive their value from an underlying asset or index.

Diluted earnings per share The earnings per share figure calculated using all potentially dilutive securities in the number of shares outstanding.

Direct method On the statement of cash flows, a method of calculating cash flow from operating activities that shows cash collections from customers; interest and dividends collected; other operating cash receipts; cash paid to suppliers and employees; interest paid; taxes paid; and other operating cash payments.

Disclaimer of opinion Independent auditor could not evaluate the fairness of the financial statements and, as a result, expresses no opinion on them.

Discontinued operations The financial results of selling a major business segment.

Discretionary items Revenues and expenses under the control of management with respect to budget levels and timing.

Dividend yield Shows the rate earned by shareholders from dividends relative to current price of stock.

Earnings before income taxes The profit recognized before the deduction of income taxes.

Earnings before interest and taxes The operating profit of a firm.

Earnings per common share Shows return to common stock shareholder for each share owned.

Earnings statement *See* Income statement.

EBITDA: The earnings before interest, taxes, depreciation, and amortization.

Equity   *See* Stockholders' equity.

Equity method   The procedure used for an investment in common stock when the investor company can exercise significant influence over the investee company; the investor recognizes investment income of the investee's net income in proportion to the percent of stock owned.

Expenses   Cost incurred to produce revenue.

Extraordinary transactions   Items that are unusual in nature and not expected to recur in the foreseeable future.

Financial Accounting Standards Board (FASB)   The private sector organization primarily responsible for establishing generally accepted accounting principles.

Financial leverage   The extent to which a firm finances with debt, measured by the relationship between total debt and total assets.

Financial ratios   Calculations made to standardize, analyze, and compare financial data; expressed in terms of mathematical relationships in the form of percentages or times.

Financial statements   Accounting information regarding the financial position of a firm, the results of operations, and the cash flows. Four statements comprise the basic set of financial statements—the balance sheet, the income statement, the statement of shareholders' equity (or the statement of retained earnings), and the statement of cash flows.

Financing activities   On the statement of cash flows, transactions that include borrowing from creditors and repaying the principal; and obtaining resources from owners and providing them with a return on the investment.

Finished goods   Products for which the manufacturing process is complete.

First in, first out (FIFO)   A method of valuing inventory and cost of goods sold under which the items purchased first are assumed to be sold first.

Fiscal year   A 12-month period starting on a date other than January 1 and ending 12 months later.

Fixed assets   Tangible, long-lived assets that are expected to provide service benefit for more than 1 year.

Fixed asset turnover   Measures efficiency of the firm in managing fixed assets.

Fixed charge coverage   Measures coverage capability more broadly than times interest earned by including operating lease payments as a fixed expense.

Foreign currency translation effects   Adjustment to the equity section of the balance sheet resulting from the translation of foreign financial statements.

Form 10-K   An annual document filed with the Securities and Exchange Commission by companies that sell securities to the public.

Form 10-Q   A quarterly document filed with the Securities and Exchange Commission by companies that sell securities to the public.

Free cash flow   A measure used by analysts to show the amount of cash available to expand, reduce debt, pay dividends, and repurchase stock; however, no standardized way to calculate this number exists.

Fulfillment costs   Expenses associated with completing an order.

Generally accepted accounting principles (GAAP)   The accounting methods and procedures used to prepare financial statements.

Goodwill   An intangible asset representing the unrecorded assets of a firm; appears in the accounting records only if the firm is acquired for a price in excess of the fair market value of its net assets.

Gross margin   *See* Gross profit.

Gross price   The full sales price of an item before any deductions are taken.

Gross profit   The difference between net sales and cost of goods sold.

Gross profit margin   Measures profit generated after consideration of cost of products sold.

Income statement   The financial statement presenting the revenues and expenses of a business enterprise for an accounting period.

Indirect method   On the statement of cash flows, a method of calculating cash flow from operating activities that shows net income adjusted for deferrals, accruals, noncash items, and non-operating items.

Industry comparisons   Average financial ratios compiled for industry groups.

Intangible assets   Assets such as goodwill that possess no physical characteristics but have value for the company.

Inventories   Items held for sale or used in the manufacture of products that will be sold.

Inventory turnover   Measures efficiency of the firm in managing and selling inventory.

Investing activities   On the statement of cash flows, transactions that include acquiring and selling, or otherwise disposing of (a) securities that are not cash equivalents and (b) productive assets that are expected to benefit the firm for long periods of time; and lending money and collecting on loans.

Investor   Someone who puts money to a use with the intent to yield a profit.

Knowledge capital   The intangible human and other factors that enable a company to earn a better than average rate of return.

Last in, first out (LIFO)   A method of valuing inventory and cost of goods sold under which the items purchased last are assumed to be sold first.

Last-in, first-out (LIFO) reserve   The difference in value between the FIFO and LIFO inventory costs when a firm uses LIFO to account for some or all of its inventory.

Leverage ratio   A ratio that measures the extent of a firm's financing with debt relative to equity and its ability to cover interest and other fixed charges.

Liabilities   Claims against assets.

Liquidity   The ability of a firm to generate sufficient cash to meet cash needs.

Liquidity ratio   A ratio that measures a firm's ability to meet needs for cash as they arise.

Long-term debt   Obligations with maturities longer than 1 year.

Long-term debt to total capitalization   Measures the extent to which long-term debt is used for permanent financing.

Lower of cost or market method   A method of valuing inventory under which cost or market, whichever is lower, is selected for each item, each group, or for the entire inventory.

Management's Discussion and Analysis of the Financial Condition and Results of Operation   A section of the annual and 10-K report that is required and monitored by the Securities and Exchange Commission in which management presents a detailed coverage of the firm's liquidity, capital resources, and operations.

Mandatorily redeemable preferred stock   Securities that have characteristics of both debt and equity.

Marketable securities   Cash not needed immediately in the business and temporarily invested to earn a return.

Matching principle   The accounting principle that requires expenses are to be matched with the generation of revenues in order to determine net income for an accounting period.

Merchandise inventories   Goods purchased for resale to the public.

Minority interest   Claims of shareholders other than the parent company against the net assets and net income of a subsidiary company.

Net earnings   The firm's profit or loss after consideration of all revenue and expense reported during the accounting period.

Net income   *See* Net earnings.

Net profit margin   Measures profit generated after consideration of all revenues and expenses.

Net revenues   *See* Net sales.

Net sales   Total sales revenue less sales returns and sales allowances.

Net trade cycle   *See* Cash conversion cycle.

Noncurrent assets/liabilities   Items expected to benefit the firm for/with maturities of more than 1 year.

Notes payable   A short-term obligation in the form of a promissory note to suppliers or financial institutions.

Notes to the financial statements   Supplementary information to financial statements that explain the firm's accounting policies and provide detail about particular accounts and other information such as pension plans.

Objectives of the analysis   The goals or purposes of analyzing, for example, a firm's financial reports.

Off-balance-sheet financing   Financial techniques for raising funds that do not have to be recorded as liabilities on the balance sheet.

Operating activities   On the statement of cash flows, transactions that include delivering or producing goods for sale and providing services; the cash effects of transactions and other events that enter into the determination of income.

Operating cycle   The time required to purchase or manufacture inventory, sell the product, and collect the cash.

Operating expenses   Costs related to the normal functions of a business.

Operating lease   A rental agreement where no ownership rights are transferred to the lessee at the termination of the rental contract.

Operating profit   Sales revenue less the expenses associated with generating sales. Operating profit measures the overall performance of a company on its normal ongoing operations.

Operating profit margin   Measures profit generated after consideration of operating expenses.

Options   *See* Stock options.

Par value   The floor price below which stock cannot be sold initially.

Payables turnover   Measures efficiency of the firm in managing accounts payable.

Permanent differences   Differences between pretax accounting income and taxable income that will cause a permanent difference between the two numbers.

Preferred stock   Capital stock of a company that carries certain privileges or rights not carried by all outstanding shares of stock.

Premature revenue recognition   Recording revenue before it should be recorded in order to increase earnings.

Prepaid expenses   Expenditures made in the current or prior period that will benefit the firm at some future time.

Price-to-earnings ratio   Expresses a multiple that the stock market places on a firm's earnings.

Pro forma earnings   Alternative earnings numbers that adjust net income in some way for items not expected to be part of ongoing business operations.

Pro forma financial statements   Projections of future financial statements based on a set of assumptions regarding future revenues, expenses, level of investment in assets, financing methods and costs, and working capital management.

Profitability ratio   A ratio that measures the overall performance of a firm and its efficiency in managing assets, liabilities, and equity.

Property, plant, and equipment   *See* Fixed assets.

Proxy statement   A statement required by the SEC used to solicit shareholder votes that also contains information about the company's directors, executives, auditors, and compensation plans.

Publicly held companies   Companies that operate to earn a profit and issue shares of stock to the public.

Qualified opinion   An opinion rendered by an independent auditor when the overall financial statements are fairly presented "except for" certain items (which the auditor discloses).

Quality of financial reporting   A subjective evaluation of the extent to which financial reporting is free of manipulation and accurately reflects the financial condition and operating success of a business enterprise.

Quick ratio   Measures short-term liquidity more rigorously than the current ratio by eliminating inventory, usually the least liquid asset.

Raw materials   Basic commodities or natural resources that will be used in the production of goods.

Reported income   The net income published in financial statements.

Reserve account   An account used in accrual accounting that allows companies to estimate and accrue obligations that will be paid in the future or estimate declines in asset values.

Restructuring charges   Costs to reorganize a company.

Retained earnings   The sum of every dollar a company has earned since its inception, less any payments made to shareholders in the form of cash or stock dividends.

Return on assets   *See* Return on investment.

Return on equity   Measures rate of return on shareholders' investment.

Return on investment   Measures overall efficiency of firm in managing assets and generating profits.

Revenue   The inflow of assets resulting from the sale of goods or services.

Sales allowance   A deduction from the original sales invoice price.

Sales return   A cancellation of a sale.

Salvage value   The amount of an asset estimated to be recoverable at the conclusion of the asset's service life.

Securities and Exchange Commission (SEC)   The public sector organization primarily responsible for establishing generally accepted accounting principles.

Segment   A component of a business enterprise that sells primarily to outside markets and for which information about revenue and profit is accumulated.

Selling, general, and administrative expenses Costs relating to the sale of products or services and to the management function of the firm.

Shareholders' equity Claims against assets by the owners of the business; represents the amount owners have invested, including income retained in the business since inception.

Short-term Generally indicates maturity of less than a year.

Statement of cash flows The financial statement that provides information about the cash inflows and outflows from operating, financing, and investing activities during an accounting period.

Statement of earnings *See* Income statement.

Statement of financial condition *See* Balance sheet.

Statement of shareholders' equity A financial statement that summarizes changes in the shareholders' equity section of the balance sheet during an accounting period.

Stock dividends and splits The issuance of additional shares of stock to existing shareholders in proportion to current ownership.

Stock options A contract that conveys the right to purchase shares of stock at a specified price within a specified time period.

Structural analysis Analysis looking at the internal structure of a business enterprise.

Taxable income The net income figure used to determine taxes payable to governments.

Temporary differences Differences between pretax accounting income and taxable income caused by reporting items of revenue or expense in one period for accounting purposes and in an earlier or later period for income tax purposes.

Times interest earned Measures how many times interest expense is covered by operating earnings.

Total asset turnover Measures efficiency of the firm in managing all assets.

Treasury stock Shares of a company's stock that are repurchased by the company and not retired.

Trend analysis Evaluation of financial data over several accounting periods.

Unqualified opinion An opinion rendered by an independent auditor of financial statements stating that the financial statements have been presented fairly in accordance with generally accepted accounting principles.

Unqualified opinion with explanatory language An opinion rendered by an independent auditor of financial statements stating that the financial statements have been presented fairly in accordance with generally accepted accounting principles, but there are items which the auditor wishes to explain to the user.

Unrealized gains (losses) on marketable equity securities The gains (losses) disclosed in the equity section resulting from the accounting rule that requires investments in marketable equity securities to be carried at the lower of cost or market value.

Vendor financing Lending money to customers so they can buy the lender's products.

Warrant A certificate issued by a corporation that conveys the right to buy a stated number of shares of stock at a specified price on or before a predetermined date.

Work-in-process Products for which the manufacturing process is only partially completed.

Working capital The amount by which current assets exceed current liabilities.

SOLUTIONS TO TEST YOURSELF

Chapter 1

1. (d)	6. (a)	11. (a)
2. (b)	7. (c)	12. (c)
3. (b)	8. (a)	13. (b)
4. (c)	9. (b)	14. (c)
5. (d)	10. (d)	

Chapter 2

1. (b)	6. (c)	11. (c)	16. (a)
2. (d)	7. (b)	12. (a)	17. (d)
3. (a)	8. (c)	13. (c)	18. (b)
4. (d)	9. (a)	14. (b)	19. (d)
5. (a)	10. (d)	15. (d)	

Chapter 3

1. (c)	6. (b)	11. (a)	16. (a)
2. (a)	7. (b)	12. (d)	17. (d)
3. (b)	8. (c)	13. (a)	18. (b)
4. (d)	9. (b)	14. (b)	
5. (a)	10. (c)	15. (c)	

Chapter 4

1. (d)	6. (c)	11. (d)
2. (b)	7. (a)	12. (b)
3. (b)	8. (d)	
4. (d)	9. (d)	
5. (a)	10. (c)	

Chapter 5

1. (b)	6. (a)	11. (a)	16. (a)
2. (c)	7. (d)	12. (b)	17. (c)
3. (d)	8. (a)	13. (c)	18. (b)
4. (c)	9. (d)	14. (c)	19. (a)
5. (b)	10. (d)	15. (d)	20. (c)

INDEX

Index

Gross margin. *See* Gross profit
Gross price, 43
Gross profit, 32
Gross profit margin, 32, 104, 105

H

Health Imaging, Eastman Kodak
Company, 94, 110, 111
Hoover's Corporate Directory, 93
Hybrid securities, 64

I

IASC. *See* International Accounting
Standards Committee
Income statement. *See* Statement
of earnings (income statement)
Income taxes, 55-56
Independent accountants, 12
Independent auditor's report in
annual reports (10-K), 12-15
Indirect method in cash flow
accounting, 75
Individual retirement accounts
(IRAs), 1
Industry comparisons, 94, 95
*Industry Norms and Key Business
Ratios,* Dun and Bradstreet
Information Services, 92
Inflows, 75, 80-81
Information sources, 90-93
auditor's report, 91
financial statements and notes, 90
form 10-K and form 10-Q, 91
Internet, 93
libraries, 92, 93
management discussion and
analysis (MD&A), 91
periodicals, 93
proxy statements, 91
supplementary schedules, 92
see also Comprehensive analysis
Infotrak-General Business Index,
92
Intangible assets, 28
Interest expense, 34
International Accounting Standards
Committee (IASC), 5
Internet, 93
Inventories, 52-55
Inventory, 31
Inventory account, 48-49
Inventory turnover, 100
Investee company (subsidiary), 35
Investing activities in statement of
cash flows, 76
Investment accounting, 35
Investor, 1, 2, 89
Investor Alert, Securities and
Exchange Commission (SEC), 2

Investor company (parent), 35
IRAs. *See* Individual retirement
accounts

K

Key financial ratios, 95-96
Kiosks, 95, 111
Kmart, 58, 84, 85
Knowledge capital, 27
"Knowledge Capital Scoreboard,"
CFO (magazine), 28
Kodak Professional, Eastman
Kodak Company, 94, 110, 111
KPMG, 13
Kynikos Associates Ltd., 20

L

Lay, Kenneth L., 17
Leases, 63
Letter to shareholders in annual
reports (10-K), 6-7
Leverage ratios, 95, 101-104
cash flow adequacy, 103-104
cash interest coverage, 103
debt ratio, 101, 102
debt to equity ratio, 102
fixed charge coverage, 103
long-term debt to total
capitalization, 102
times interest earned, 102
Levitt, Arthur, 4, 14
Liabilities, 49, 58-64
commitments and
contingencies, 63-64
common size balance sheets,
54-55
current liabilities, 58
hybrid securities, 64
long-term borrowings, 59
other long-term liabilities, 62-63
payables, 58
postemployment liabilities, 59-62
shareholders' equity, 49, 64-66
short-term borrowings, 58
taxes and dividends payable, 59
total liabilities, 64
see also Shareholders' equity;
Statement of financial
condition (balance sheet)
Libraries, 92, 93
LIFO (last-in, first-out), 31, 53
LIFO reserve, 53
Limited partnerships, Enron
Corporation, 60
Liquidity analysis, 49
Liquidity ratios, 95, 96-99
average collection period, 98
cash flow liquidity ratio, 97
current ratio, 96-97

days inventory held, 98-99
days payable outstanding, 99
net trade cycle, 99
quick ratio, 97
Long-term debt, 59
Long-term debt to total
capitalization ratio, 102
Long-term liabilities, 62-63
Long-term receivables and other
noncurrent assets, 57-58
Lower of cost or market method,
121
Lucent Technologies, 6

M

Management creativity, 27
Management discussion and
analysis (MD&A), 91
in annual reports (10-K), 15
Eastman Kodak Company, 15,
30, 32, 33, 34, 39, 81
Manditorily redeemable preferred
stock, 64
*Manufacturing U.S.A. Industry
Analyses,* Gale Research Inc.,
92
Marginal companies, 2
Marketable securities, 35, 51
Market price data, Eastman
Kodak Company, 17
Market ratios, 107-108
Market Share Reporter, Gale
Research Inc., 93
Matching principle, 25-26
MCI Center in Washington, 116
MD&A. *See* Management
discussion and analysis
Merchandise inventories, 121
*Mergent Manuals and Mergent
Handbook,* Moody's Investor
Service, 93
Microsoft Excel, 93
MicroStrategy, 44
"Mind the Gap," *CFO* (magazine),
79
Minority interest, 121
Moody's Investor Service, *Mergent
Manuals and Mergent
Handbook,* 93
Morningstar Mutual Funds, 93
Motorola, 44, 72-74, 94
Multex Investor, 93
Mutual funds, 93

N

NASDAQ, 2-3, 43
Net earnings, 34-35, 37
Net profit margin, 34-35
Net revenues, 30